Federal-State Relations in Sabah, Malaysia

The **Institute of Southeast Asian Studies (ISEAS)** was established as an autonomous organization in 1968. It is a regional centre dedicated to the study of socio-political, security and economic trends and developments in Southeast Asia and its wider geostrategic and economic environment. The Institute's research programmes are the Regional Economic Studies (RES, including ASEAN and APEC), Regional Strategic and Political Studies (RSPS), and Regional Social and Cultural Studies (RSCS).

ISEAS Publications, an established academic press, has issued more than 1,000 books and journals. It is the largest scholarly publisher of research about Southeast Asia from within the region. ISEAS Publications works with many other academic and trade publishers and distributors to disseminate important research and analyses from and about Southeast Asia to the rest of the world.

Federal-State Relations in Sabah, Malaysia

The Berjaya Administration, 1976-85

REGINA LIM

INSTITUTE OF SOUTHEAST ASIAN STUDIES
Singapore

First published in Singapore in 2008 by
ISEAS Publishing
Institute of Southeast Asian Studies
30 Heng Mui Keng Terrace
Pasir Panjang Road
Singapore 119614

Internet e-mail: publish@iseas.edu.sg
World Wide Web: <http://bookshop.iseas.edu.sg>

ISEAS Library Cataloguing-in-Publication Data

Lim, Regina.
Federal-state relations in Sabah, Malaysia: the Berjaya administration, 1976–85.
1. Sabah—Politics and government—20th century.
2. Sabah—History—20th century.
3. Central-local government relations—Malaysia.
4. Federal government—Malaysia.
5. Parti Berjaya.
I. Title.
DS597.336 L73 2008

ISBN 978-981-230-811-5 (soft cover)
ISBN 978-981-230-812-2 (hard cover)
ISBN 978-981-230-813-9 (PDF)

Typeset by International Typesetters Pte Ltd
Printed in Singapore by Photoplates Private Limited

CONTENTS

LIST OF TABLES AND FIGURES

ACKNOWLEDGEMENTS

In the research, preparation, and writing of this book, I benefited enormously from the advice, consultation and tolerance of Professor Francis Loh Kok Wah of the School of Social Sciences, Universiti Sains Malaysia (USM), who supervised the original postgraduate research on which this is based. I also want to thank Dr Lim Hong Hai of the School of Social Science, USM, for his critical but constructive comments. In Sabah, I would also like to express my appreciation to the staff of the Sabah Archives, the Sabah State Library, and the Research Library at Yayasan Sabah; all of whom were efficient and helpful in the services they provided. In Singapore, the staff at the Singapore/Malaysia Collection of the National University of Singapore Library were likewise extremely helpful. To all those who consented to be interviewed, I express my sincere thanks. I also made use of the Malaysian Hansard records collected by Dr Rochana Bajpai of the School of Oriental and African Studies, London, under a research grant from Balliol College, Oxford, and I wish to record my appreciation to her for allowing me access to these sources. I am very grateful to the School of Social Science and the Department of Political Science and International Studies at the University of Birmingham for funding my trip to Singapore to present some of the findings of this book at the 2nd Singapore Graduate Forum 2007, organized by the Asia Research Institute of the National University of Singapore; participant comments were also gratefully received.

Special acknowledgements for support and encouragement must go to my husband, Graham, the eternal optimist, and to my son, Nick, who provided essential distraction, both when it was needed and when it was not. I would also like to express my appreciation to Nancy, Japiril, James Lim Ching Ping and Matirissiah for their generous logistical and familial support, enabling the book to be finally completed. Last but not least, I would like to dedicate this book to my late father, Lim Ah Nick (1925–95), whose living memory of North Borneo and Sabah was the most precious inheritance that I have received, and which has enriched my life and the lives of others who knew him well.

ABBREVIATIONS AND GLOSSARY OF TERMS

ABIM	Angkatan Belia Islam Malaysia, Islamic Youth Movement of Malaysia
ABC System	System of granting political reward in the BERJAYA party
ACNA	Advisory Council for Native Affairs
Adat	Indigenous social customs and laws
Amanah Rakyat Sabah	Annual dividends distributed by the Sabah Foundation for Sabahans who were 21 years of age and above
Anak	Child
Bapa	Father
BERJAYA	Parti Bersatu Rakyat Jelata Sabah, United Sabah People's Party
BERSATU	Koperasi Usaha Bersatu Malaysia Sdn Bhd
Bersih, Cekap, Amanah	Clean, Efficient, Honest (BN campaign slogan)
BN	Barisan Nasional, National Front
BNBC	British North Borneo Company
Bobohizan	Native Kadazan-Dusun priestess
BPU	*Bumiputera* Participation Unit
bumiputera	Indigenous people
CDO	Community Development Officer
CPA	Commonwealth Parliamentary Association
Dakwah	Islamic missionary activity
DAP	Democratic Action Party
Datu	Independent chiefs or leaders in the Sulu System
EC	Election Commission of Malaysia
Huguan Siou	Kadazan-Dusun Paramount Chief
IGC	Intergovernmental Committee
Jajahan	System of territorial governance under the Brunei Sultanate

JKK	Jawatankuasa Kemajuan Kampung, Village Development Committee
JKKK	Jawatankuasa Keselamatan dan Kemajuan Kampung, Village Security and Development Committee
JUB	Syarikat Jaya Usaha Bersatu Sdn Bhd
Kaamatan	Kadazan-Dusun Harvest Festival
Khalwat	Illicit proximity between a man and a woman
KMA	Kinabalu Motor Assembly
KOBERSA	Koperasi BERJAYA Berhad
KOJASA	Koperasi Jelata Sabah
KO-NELAYAN	Koperasi Serbaguna Nelayan Sabah
KORAS	Koperasi Rakyat Sabah
KOSAN	SANYA Multi-purpose Cooperative Bhd
KOSMA	KOSAN Marketing Agency
KPD	Koperasi Pembangunan Desa
MSC	Malaysian Solidarity Convention
MSCC	Malaysian Solidarity Consultative Committee
MUIS	Majlis Ugama Islam Sabah, Sabah Islamic Council
NCAC	Native Chief Advisory Council
ODA	Overbeck-Dent Association
Orang Tua	Village Headman (lit. Elder)
PAP	People's Action Party
PAS	Partai Islam SeMalaysia, Pan-Malaysian Islamic Party
Pasok Momogun	National Pasok Momogun Organization
PBS	Parti Bersatu Sabah, Sabah United Party
PBBS	Persatuan Brunei *Bumiputera* Sabah, Sabah Association of Brunei *Bumiputera*
PERKIM	Pertubuhan Kebajikan Islam Malaysia, Muslim Welfare Organization of Malaysia
Perkina	Perusahaan Kinabalu Motor
PKR	Pemimpin Kemajuan Rakyat, People's Development Leaders
PSBB	Persatuan Sabah Bajau Bersatu, Sabah United Association of Bajau
PBB	*Pribumi* Participation Unit
Pribumi	Muslim and non-Muslim indigenous people in Sabah
Pusat Latihan Dakwah	*Dakwah* Training Centre
SAFODA	Sabah Forest Development Authority

SAMA	Sabah Marketing Cooperative Bhd
SANYA	Sabah National Youth Association
SCA	Sabah Chinese Association
SCCP	Sabah Chinese Consolidated Party
SEB	Sabah Electricity Board
SEDCO	Sabah Economic Development Corporation
SKCA	Sabah Kadazan Cultural Association
SLDB	Sabah Land Development Board
Tamu	Weekly market in major villages in Sabah
Tapai	Rice wine
Towkay	Influential Chinese businessman
Tulin	Part of a river governed by independent chiefs or officers of the Brunei Sultanate
UMNO	United Malays National Organization
UNKO	United National Kadazan Organization
UPKO	United National Pasok Momogun Organization
USDA	United Sabah Dusun Association
USIA	United Sabah Islamic Association
USNO	United Sabah National Organization
YPS	Yayasan Pribumi Sabah, Sabah Native's Foundation

1

INTRODUCTION

This book aims to bridge an understanding of the politics of the Malaysian state of Sabah within the broader spectrum of the country's political system and development. As one of the two Malaysian states on the island of Borneo, along with neighbouring Sarawak, Sabah is separated from the West Malaysian peninsula by a thousand kilometres of the South China Sea. Moreover, both states also have historical legacies and cultural and political endowments vastly at odds from West Malaysia. To take one simple but important example, the common ethno-demographic characterization of Malaysia as divided into a Malay/*bumiputera* majority, and Chinese and Indian minorities may be essentially accurate in political, if not anthropological, terms for West Malaysia, but falls far short of capturing the political complexities of ethnic diversity in Sabah and Sarawak. Politics and political parties in Sabah hence tend to be less 'racialized' (Mandal 2004) and the communal model of party politics, which is so often the focus of interest in comparative studies of Malaysia (e.g. Horowitz 1985; Lijphart 1977), is consequently considerably less entrenched in Sabah. Historically, state elections in Sabah have produced an absolute majority for a single party that claimed 'multi-ethnic' status in six consecutive elections between 1976 and 1994. In West Malaysia, prior to the surprise results of the March 2008 elections, only Penang had come anywhere close to this and then only once, with the victory of the nominally multi-ethnic Gerakan party in 1969, which subsequently entered the *Barisan Nasional* (BN, or National Front) coalition.

Despite these manifest differences, Sabah and Sarawak are often under-explored or virtually ignored in mainstream analyses of the country's political system. Broad analyses of Malaysian politics that routinely appear on undergraduate reading lists (e.g. Case 1996; Crouch 1996*a*; Means 1991), while interesting and insightful in their own ways, are often primarily or exclusively studies of West Malaysia. Sabah and Sarawak are largely ignored in Malaysian political studies, primarily because they do not conform to the conventional perspectives of ethnic politics found in West Malaysia.

This oversight is all the more glaring because not only do Sabah and Sarawak constitute a significant proportion of the total population of Malaysia, but they have historically been assigned considerably greater electoral weight at the national level than their equivalent population share (see Table 1.1). There is clearly something of an imbalance here. While academic and non-academic analysts of the broad politics of Malaysia tend to underplay the importance of Sabah and Sarawak, the custodians of the country's formal political system — the nominally independent but politically subservient Election Commission (EC) — have granted it continuous over-representation. This book attempts to rectify that imbalance somewhat and, given the author's current lack of influence with the EC either now or in the foreseeable future, the most appropriate path by which to do so is an attempt to address the left-hand side of the equation by contributing to an enrichment of our understanding of the political dynamics of Sabah.

In seeking to provide an understanding of the political dynamics in Sabah in such a way that will hopefully enrich broader political analyses of Malaysia, this book focuses primary attention on a relatively short period of time, specifically the period between 1976 and 1985, when the State Administration was controlled by the multi-ethnic *Parti Bersatu Rakyat Jelata Sabah* (BERJAYA). There are two main reasons for this focus. Firstly, as will become clear through the following chapters, I will argue that this was the period in which the broad 'rules of the game' in Sabah solidified, particularly with respect to the nature of the relationship between Sabah as a state and the

Table 1.1
Electoral Weight of East Malaysian States in the Federal Parliament, 1974–2004

	1974	1984	1994	2004
Percentage of electorate	14.7	15.0	16.8	16.5
Percentage of seats	26.0	25.5	25.0	25.7
Over-weightage (ratio)	1.77	1.70	1.49	1.56

Source: Brown (2005); figures for 2004 updated following redelimitation exercise in Sarawak.

Federal political system dominated by the *Barisan Nasional* coalition. While the preceding and subsequent periods of political development in the state have undoubtedly seen periods of turbulence, uncertainty and high political drama, it was precisely the relative political quiescence of Sabah during the BERJAYA period that demands our attention.

The second reason for a focus on the BERJAYA period is somewhat more prosaic. While a number of scholars have analysed both the preceding administration led by the United Sabah National Organization (USNO, 1967–76) and the succeeding *Parti Bersatu Sabah* (PBS, or Sabah United Party, 1985–94) Administration (Brown 2004; Luping 1994; Means 1968; Milne 1973; Milne and Ratnam 1974), considerably less work has been done on the BERJAYA Administration itself. Sabah has attracted some scholarly attention since 1985, when 'Kadazan nationalism' saw the state swing politically, but these analyses have done so against a largely blank historical slate (Kahin 1992; Loh 1992; Puthucheary 1985). Such attention that has been paid to BERJAYA has tended to focus on the dramatic events surrounding its birth and rise to power in the period, 1975–76, or else its sudden fall from grace in the period 1984–85 (Han 1979; Loh 1992; Ramanathan 1986; Tilman 1976). No significant work has focused on the style and nature of the BERJAYA Administration, particularly in relation to the political fusion engendered by the institution of Federal authority over the Sabah State Government through the process of party politics during the BERJAYA Administration.

There are two broad and important processes that I will highlight in this book: (1) the historical transformations of the administrative system, and (2) the role of party politics in blurring the contours of governance and politics in Sabah in the modern era. In the official history of Sabah, North Borneo experienced colonialism under the BNBC, witnessed local resistance, particularly from Mat Salleh and the Rundum Rebellion, that was violently put down at the turn of the century, endured the Japanese Occupation, and was subsequently ceded to the Crown Colony's administration prior to the formation of the Malaysian Federation in 1963. From 1881 till today, Sabah has therefore experienced four different types of administration: (1) by a chartered trading company, the British North Borneo Company (BNBC), (2) the Japanese Military Administration, (3) as a British Crown Colony in 1946, and (4) as part of the the Malaysian Federation since 1963. Some historians of Sabah, particularly the late James Ongkili (1981; 1972; 1985), have tended to view North Borneo history as beginning with the BNBC whilst others, such as Ranjit Singh (1980; 2000), have been more inclined to trace the historical roots of North Borneo within the context of the negotiation of local agents with the colonizing Europeans. Whilst the BNBC provides a more substantive documentation of North Borneo history, it is also important to critically reflect upon these official discourses and reconstruct our understanding in relation to the role of historical agents in shaping the outcome of political negotiations. It is within this context of negotiation, between the local agents and those who came to 'cheer up' the life-world of Sabah, that the historical processes have been embellished, affecting the evolution and development of the structure of the administration and its politics.

The most significant change that affected the administration of Sabah was the formation of the Malaysian Federation in 1963. Under the administration of the British Crown Colony, the first District Council election was held in December 1962 and, under the Malaysian Federation, the first election for the Legislative Assembly took place in April 1967. The electoral process and political parties were therefore introduced in a context of rapid changes brought about by the creation of Malaysia (Milne and Ratnam 1974). In his personal correspondence to the British Prime Minister, Lord Cobbold, the chair of the committee mandated by Malaya and Britain to explore the possibility of merging North Borneo, Sarawak and Singapore with Malaya, expressed concerns that Kuala Lumpur "might make a mess of the Borneo territories in the early years".[1] The political crises during the early years of the Sabah Alliance illustrated the 'messiness' that plagued political development in Sabah at the beginning of the Malaysian Federation. This may in part be attributed to the superficial understanding on the part of the elites in Kuala Lumpur with regard to the ethnic diversity and local conditions in Sabah, and partly to the on-going political struggle of the political elites in Sabah in coming to terms with the experience of governing a new state in a new federation.

This book attempts to clarify some of that 'messiness' and examine the political development of Sabah from pre-independence until 1985. The principal argument that I propose is that Sabah politics has indeed been 'messy' but that this 'messiness' can be understood if we adopt a framework which gives attention to the often contradictory pressures affecting the process of negotiation in the multiple domains of power relations within the Malaysian Federation. Within the Malaysian Federation system, there are on-going tensions affecting the State Administration and involving state politicians in a 'negotiation processes' between the 'ethnic' demands of local politics and the political expectations of the Federal Government, in the context of rapid modernization. The Malaysian Federation as it was formed in 1963 consisted of fourteen territorial states: eleven states in West Malaysia, two in the Borneo territories of Sabah and Sarawak, and Singapore, which separated from Malaysia in 1965. Sabah and Sarawak are electorally over-represented, constituting around a quarter of Parliamentary seats despite making up barely sixteen per cent of the electorate. When the Malaysia project was proposed, Tunku Abdul Rahman had apparently made up his mind about how the native (non-Chinese) people of Borneo would be able to defuse the threat of the dominant Chinese in Singapore against the Malay position (Stockwell 2004). Without the natives of North Borneo and Sarawak, the bilateral merger of Malaya and Singapore would result in an increase in the percentage of Chinese in the population to 45 per cent against the Malay population at only 42.3 per cent. The inclusion of the Borneo territories would thus increase the overall number of natives which the Malays could claim to represent and so become politically dominant in the new federation against the Chinese communities. Stockwell added that, "the Tunku was misled into believing that the peoples of Brunei, North Borneo and Sarawak would welcome his intervention. In fact he soon encountered antagonism from local leaders who were suspicious of a stratagem which threatened to replace one colonial regime with another and to subordinate their rights and interests to those of Kuala Lumpur" (Stockwell 2004, p. ixx).

Sabah politics, particularly its relation with the Federal Government in Kuala Lumpur, began to descend into 'messiness' on two important historical events: firstly, when Tunku Abdul Rahman intervened to 'resolve' inter-party rivalry between USNO and UPKO and, secondly, when Tunku Abdul Rahman expelled Singapore in 1965 without consulting the leaders of Sabah and Sarawak. The Chief Ministers and leaders of the largest non-Muslim native communities in Sabah and Sarawak — Donald Stephens representing the Kadazan community and Stephen Kalong Ningkan representing the Dayak/Iban community respectively — fervently protested the unilateral decision of Tunku Abdul Rahman. Their requests for a referendum under international auspices were met with a hostile reaction from the Federal Government. State autonomy has since become a thorny issue surrounding the relations between Kuala Lumpur and Sabah, and to some extent, Sarawak. Much as the Federal Government tried to maintain a viable political system within the Federation, the manner with which Tunku Abdul Rahman negotiated local affairs in Sabah and Sarawak had been questionable. Means (1968) demonstrated the extent to which Tunku Abdul Rahman had personally intervened in favour of the Muslim leader against the incumbent Chief Minister (non-Muslim) during the Sabah Alliance crisis, and how Tunku Abdul Rahman had encouraged the formation of a pro-Malay 'Native Alliance' with the purpose of dismissing Stephen Kalong Ningkan from the Sarawak State Government. When the first motion on the 'vote of no confidence' against Ningkan was dismissed by the High Court in Sarawak, a State of Emergency was declared on 14 September 1966, giving emergency powers to the Parliament under Clause 150 of The Federal Constitution of Malaysia, and transferring all state powers to the federal authorities to amend the Sarawak Constitution.[2]

Singapore's expulsion and Kuala Lumpur's early political intervention in Sabah and Sarawak illustrated the significance of Federal control over the issues of state autonomy in State Administration and party politics in East Malaysia. For the Federal Government, the universal idea of a Malaysian nation must prevail over regional sentiments and it therefore seemed only natural that the West Malaysian model of administration and party politics be extended to Sabah and Sarawak. "We must have somebody responsible as Chief Minister who will try to make himself a Malaysian and not perpetuate colonial rule".[3] This was an indication that the process of 'Malayanization' in the State Administration and party politics should proceed at a pace that was sanctioned by the Federal Government and in a manner that would not court the attention of the international community, especially after the '*Konfrontasi*' affair, when Indonesian President Sukarno initiated low-level military engagement in Borneo to protest what he saw as the illegitimacy of the Malaysia proposal. However, politics in Sabah was conditioned by different kinds of social forces that did not necessarily conform to the distinct communal boundaries found in the Peninsula. The uncertainties of ethno-religious constellations among the population in Sabah were in stark contrast to the relatively more structured ethnic identifications in the Peninsula. Sabah's complex ethnicity could not be resolved through the Alliance model à la West Malaysian politics. But one way of bringing the complexity of Sabah's ethnicity within the conceptual grasp of the Federal Government would involve the rationalization of the Sabah State Administration through delimiting the liberty of party politics to the confines of the *Barisan Nasional* coalition. It was therefore imperative for the Federal Government to be politically assertive when it came to taming the growing pains of a new territory that gained independence under its guardianship.

Despite severe ethnic differences, Malaysia has one of the best post-Second World War growth records in the world and has successfully avoided major conflict. Yet anything more than a cursory examination of Malaysia would reveal the extent to which ethnicity and, indeed, ethnic tensions are fundamental to an understanding of the country's historical development and contemporary political climate. Malaysia is constitutionally a federal democracy with regular elections carried out both at the Parliamentary level as well as the local State Legislative Assembly level. Parliamentary elections will determine the composition of the Federal House of Representatives, who are responsible for the deliberation on any constitutional amendment. Kuala Lumpur and Putrajaya, formerly in the state of Selangor, and Labuan, formerly in the state of Sabah, have been made Federal Territories which come under the direct administration of the Federal Government and Parliamentary elections for the Federal House of Representatives. State elections for the State Legislative Assembly are now carried out in tandem with the Parliamentary election, although Sabah and Sarawak have had State elections occur at different times from the Parliamentary elections, especially from the 1970s till the 1990s.[4] Since the abolition of elective local government in Malaysia in 1973, State elections for the Legislative Assembly have become important channels for the local population to express their views and concerns about local issues. Local issues remain considerably important for the Sabah electorate, and these have often contributed to the changes of Sabah State Governments via elections.

Sabah is the only state in Malaysia that has experienced four different political parties governing the state, beginning with the USNO-led Sabah Alliance (1967–76), and followed by BERJAYA (1976–85), the *Parti Bersatu Sabah* (1985–94) and, currently, the UMNO-led coalition. In examining the historical trajectories of Sabah politics, it is important to identify the processes that have enabled UMNO to gain a strong foothold in the Sabah State Government. As the first party to govern Sabah after independence, USNO, in many ways, resembled the regime aspiration of UMNO. However, many scholars have illustrated the disparity of USNO's Islamist policies against local ethnic demands and conditions. Although there has not been much scholarly attention paid to BERJAYA, these studies tend to highlight the similarities of BERJAYA's Islamist policies to the USNO regime. In many ways, USNO and BERJAYA had many similarities in their Islamic outlook; however, there were also considerable contestations and enmity between the two parties, particularly in relation to competing for political support from the Federal Government and in negotiating their Islamic credentials in the eyes of Muslim communities in Sabah. BERJAYA was also caught in the peculiar situation of having to sell its 'multiracial' appeal to the non-Muslim communities and this makes it an interesting case study of how a local State Government had to juggle between the demands of a strong Federal Government against the tide of local social forces. In the history of local State elections in Sabah, these social forces had been responsible for the many facets of change in the Sabah State Government. From USNO to BERJAYA, and its ultimate political downfall in 1985, popular discontent against BERJAYA's policies became the bone of contention among the Sabah voters. But the difference between USNO's downfall and that of BERJAYA was that PBS was a party that was not politically engineered by the Federal Government. It was a party that was rooted in the groundswell of political discontent articulated against the BERJAYA State Government by the people of Sabah.

In the contemporary politics of Malaysia, the BN now effectively controls the electoral machine, funding and media, which almost always guarantees substantial majorities for the government in the Parliamentary and most State elections (e.g. Crouch 1996*b*; Khoo 2005). Some writers have even argued that the Election Commission has frequently redrawn election/constituency boundaries in Sabah and Sarawak for the purpose of demarcating the electorates into more structured ethno-religious affiliations. Loh (2003) has also argued that the existence of "phantom" voters has tilted the Sabah electorates in favour of the BN since the elections in the 1990s.

While the BN now possesses technological superiority in mobilizing what Loh (2003) called the 3 Ms (Machinery, Money and Media), there are a number of issues that remain prickly within the coalition. Harold Crouch contended that each constituent party within the BN coalition would still need to win more seats to augment their bargaining position against other political parties within the coalition and, in order to achieve this, individual political parties will need to be responsive to grassroots' aspirations and expectations (Crouch 1996*a*, p. 55).

Chapter 2 reconstructs an understanding of North Borneo history. It argues the common perception that Sabah's political development 'began' in 1881 with the formation of the BNBC is inaccurate, and that the evolution of governance in Sabah during the colonial period was very much a negotiation between BNBC and local agents in a way that very much prefigures the kind of tensions that emerged between the Federal Government and local politicians in the post-colonial era.

Chapter 3 traces the political tensions affecting the relations between Kuala Lumpur and Sabah at the point of entry into the Malaysian Federation, and Singapore's unprecedented expulsion from the Federation. It looks at how the political crises and regime change at the Federal level redefined the character of party politics shaping Federal-State relations between Kuala Lumpur and Sabah as well as politics at the local setting. This chapter provides an insight into the political background of Sabah's entry into the Federation and demonstrates the extent to which early Federal intervention in the local administration and ethnic politics in Sabah contributed to a political 'mess', prompting the creation of the BERJAYA party.

Chapter 4 illustrates the extent to which the political rivalry between USNO and BERJAYA was considerably linked to the intra-party factionalism within UMNO as well as the inter-party competition between PAS and UMNO in the BN coalition. It also discusses the ways in which BERJAYA encouraged and facilitated the process of restructuring some of the government departments in Sabah under Federal jurisdiction. This chapter also presents the grey area in which party political bargaining could result in the federalization of local state departments and Labuan Island.

Chapter 5 discusses BERJAYA's development policies and the way they were linked to political support for the party. Due to the existence of opposition areas, some development packages became highly selective and politicized. This chapter presents how BERJAYA utilized the cooperative movements to facilitate the economic development of rural areas, and also highlights the high profile court case involving JKKK's role in politicizing the dispensation of development packages to the villages.

Chapter 6 analyses the peculiar situation of BERJAYA in mediating the thorny issue of ethnicity and religion in Sabah. This chapter also exposes the crux of the problem that any Sabah State Government will have to resolve, and how the BERJAYA period demonstrated an interesting case in the 'tug-of-war' between the demands of an Islamic administration at the Federal level against the multiple domains of local issues affecting the heterogeneous population in Sabah.

Chapter 7 concludes with discussion of the post-BERJAYA period.

Notes

1 Lord Cobbold to [Secretary of State for the Colonies] Maudling, 9 March 1962, CO 1030/987, no. E/1128.

2 The State of Emergency was declared on the grounds of communist insurgency in Sarawak and also to prevent the prospect of the *Council Negeri* being dissolved by Ningkan to hold an election (Means 1968).

3 *Straits Times*, 26 September 1966 (cited in Means 1966).

4 During the 2004 and 2008 general elections in Malaysia, the Sabah State election was carried out in tandem with the Parliamentary election.

2

SABAH BEFORE MALAYSIA

INTRODUCTION

James Ongkili, a native Kadazan historian of Sabah and politician who figured prominently in the BERJAYA Administration, once described North Borneo before the founding of the British North Borneo Company in 1881 as a geographical realm with "no community, no overall administration, no State economy, no State government ... only mountains, jungles, rivers and the surrounding seas, and isolated villages scattered over the more than 29,000 square miles of tropical and warm equatorial land" (Ongkili 1981, p. xxvii). Indeed, these remarks were made in his introduction to a *Commemorative History of Sabah*, sponsored by the BERJAYA State Government as part of a 'centenary' celebration. For Ongkili and, implicitly, the State Administration in which he was the senior cabinet 'representative' of the native, non-Muslim ethnic groups, the history of Sabah *began* with colonialism — a sentiment markedly at odds with the intellectual and political discourse of nationalists in West Malaysia and beyond, who are usually at pains to emphasize the glory of pre-colonial political systems such as, in the West Malaysian case, the Sultanate of Melaka (Brown 2007; cf. Smith 1999).

Before Western colonialism, the Brunei Sultanate was a major power in the region, controlling substantial portions of Borneo and southern parts of the Philippine archipelago. However, the Brunei Sultanate began to lose its territories between 1840 and 1890 as a result of the expansionist policies of the Brooke regime in Sarawak and the presence of British North Borneo Company (BNBC). The rapid 'dismemberment' of Brunei therefore happened through the process of the cession of many rivers, except for the Limbang

River which was annexed by the Brooke regime in 1890 — an occupation that the Brunei Sultan has never legally conceded till today (Tarling 1971; Wright 1970).

The first British foothold in what later became British North Borneo came in 1847, when Britain acquired the island of Labuan from Brunei to promote two main purposes: (1) the establishment of a naval base to suppress piracy and to protect its trading routes between Singapore and the ports of China, and (2) the exploitation of island's coal deposits (Galbraith 1965; Tarling 1978). When two colonial entrepreneurs, Baron von Overbeck and Alfred Dent, expressed their interest in acquiring trading rights in North Borneo, it generated an opportunity for the British to reconsider their strategic position against other European powers present in the region in renegotiating their borders of control on areas that were still under the suzerainty of the Brunei and Sulu Sultanates. As the power structures of the Sultanates weakened in the wake of a growing European mercantilist monopoly in the region, the British took this opportunity to consolidate their imperial position, giving the BNBC a legal foothold in North Borneo.

The BNBC played a crucial role in the history of state formation in North Borneo through the implementation of a modern administrative system. The presence of a colonial administration altered the traditional structures of authority, with considerable implications upon social relations in native society in Sabah. These changes, however, did not appeal to the native population and a number of protests and violent rebellions emerged, notably the Mat Salleh Revolt during the period 1895–1903 and the Rundum Rebellion during the period 1900–15. After these revolts, the BNBC instituted a system of native administration with the aim of establishing a consultative body of Native Chiefs to facilitate an effective dialogue between the BNBC and the leaders of the various districts in North Borneo until 1941. However, the progress of native participation in political dialogue was interrupted during the Japanese Occupation. The system was again revived after the war under the Crown Colony Administration. North Borneo and Labuan were thus ceded to the British Crown in 1946 following the post-war financial losses incurred by the BNBC. Under the British Crown, Sabah was grouped with Brunei and Sarawak to form the British Borneo Territories. A Governor was appointed to administer each of the territories, which came under the jurisdiction of the Commissioner-General for Southeast Asia, based in Malaya. The administrative reforms during this period were moving towards the formation of a modern political state, which would undertake planned economic development and the provision of better social services to raise the general standard of living of the population in North Borneo.

PRE-COLONIAL NORTH BORNEO

It is not easy to reconstruct an understanding of the history of North Borneo but a number of avenues and ways of thinking will be sought in its interpretation. In capturing these issues, Anthony Reid (1993) had elucidated a typology of modernities exemplified through the emergence of states in pre-colonial Southeast Asia via increased regional trade relations, the centralizing forces of classical states, and the spread and localization of world religions — particularly in the form of archaeological evidence of temples, shrines and court chronicles confirming the early influences of Hinduism and Islam. Hence, long before European mercantilist incursion into Southeast Asia, the classical states in the Southeast Asian archipelago — Srivijaya, Majapahit, Aceh, Banten, and Melaka — exemplified some of these modernizing features in the sixteenth century, attesting to the indigenous development of early states and civilizations pre-dating Western colonialism.

Wolters (1999; 1994), on the other hand, prefered a different tack when it comes to understanding the cultural and historical diversity of the region. Instead of searching for an ancient kingdom, Wolters suggested the possibility of other forms of power centre that did not necessarily share the features of classical states. He suggested the importance of understanding the role of culture and kinship in Southeast Asia in shaping the rise and the continuity of powerful leaders or 'men of prowess' within a specific locality. Wolters conceptualized power from the perspective of the 'big men' or 'men of prowess' on "their being attributed with an abnormal amount of personal and innate 'soul stuff', that distinguished their leadership qualities from that of others in their generation and especially among their own kinsmen" (Wolters 1999, p. 18). This perspective therefore gives more flexibility in thinking about societies or even communities that draw upon oral histories and collective memories as ways of keeping their histories relevant to their existing cultures.

How these powerful leaders came about may differ from one society to another but their control over people or a population seemed to be the shared feature that defined their source of political power. In his exploration of the Malay *Kerajaan*, Anthony Milner argued that the Malays "considered themselves to be living not in so many states but under individual Rajas" and described the Raja's political power in terms of generating wealth for the purpose of "forming sizeable personal following" (Milner 1982, p. 9). In analysing the indigenous political system of Western Malaya, Gullick argued that "where land is not a scarce commodity, as in the case of the Malay States, political power even though it is exercised in respect of defined territorial areas is based on control of people" (Gullick 1989, p. 113). Walker (2002) defined Malay power in nineteenth century Sarawak as a process of wealth creation with the aim of developing entourages and followers to support the logistics of trade expansions and periodic warfare. The lesser-known states or 'port polities' in the Malay Peninsula, along the coasts of Borneo, Java, Sulawesi, and the islands of Moluccas and Mindanao, therefore provided the basis for the role of local agents and their involvement in trade as instrumental for certain forms of socio-political organizations to emerge in the pre-colonial era (Kathirithamby-Wells and Villiers 1990). Maguin (1991) argued that commerce played a substantial role in shaping the early phases of coastal, harbour-centred political systems, although he also acknowledged the extent to which the merchant class (*orangkaya*) "could both do and undo a king" (1991, p. 51), especially when these wealthy chiefs were able to attract large numbers of political followers. The power relations between the ruler and the ruled therefore impinged upon the ability of the ruler in establishing political alliances and networks with the wealthy and powerful local chiefs. Walker (2002, p. 26) illustrated how the prosperity of local chiefs who controlled the Sarawak River in the nineteenth century began to undermine the commercial viability of the Brunei Sultanate, and how the subsequent political intervention from the Brunei court prompted the Sarawak Malays to revolt in 1836.

Abinales and Amoroso (2005) emphasized the pivotal role of *Datu*, as an example of 'men of prowess', in shaping social relations and stratification in pre-colonial Philippines society, and the extent to which these *Datu* established political alliances to the Sulu Sultanate. The distinctive lifestyle and entourages of the *Datu*, both within their household and among their rank-and-file followers in the public sphere, portrayed significant attributes of power within their immediate environment. The people who were not directly linked to the entourage of a *Datu* would normally come into contact with him via tribute or some form of servitude in times of hardship, capture or criminal offence. This form of social contact or relation also underlined the role of these powerful leaders in dealing with one of the most lucrative trades at that time which was slave trading, a system of bondage that constituted a very significant cultural element in the history of Southeast Asia. Abinales and Amoroso had therefore shifted the conventional perspective from the search for an ancient state to an emphasis on understanding how local cultural practices define the perception of power, and how such perception reinforces the existing social as well as power relations within a particular society. In the case of North Borneo, the Brunei and Sulu Sultanates provided a semblance of political establishment and control through local agents in parts of North

Borneo and Sarawak under its suzerainty. However, it is the pivotal role of these local agents, which reflected their attempts, on the one hand, to make sense of the new colonial order and, on the other hand, to resist further erosion of their traditional power, that will give shape and meaning to the current understanding of the history of North Borneo.

THE BRUNEI *JAJAHAN* AND THE *DATU* SYSTEM IN THE SULU ARCHIPELAGO

The historical development of a modern administrative structure in North Borneo could be traced to the changes that occurred within the old ruling establishments of the Brunei-Sulu Sultanate. Historians of Southeast Asia have documented the extent to which the river systems contributed to the emergence of early states within the indigenous system (Stark and Allen 1998), and the geographically strategic importance of rivers for upstream-downstream jungle trade and cultural exchanges as well as political control (Cleary 1996; Andaya 1993; Hall 2001; Walker 2002). Ranjit Singh (1990) suggested that port-hinterland relations in the form of the *Jajahan* system of the Brunei Sultanate on the West coast and the *Datu* system of the Sulu Sultanate on the East coast of Sabah were the earliest forms of governing structures existing before the BNBC takeover. These political structures were established along the coastal plains, whereas the interior regions of Sabah remained relatively independent from their control. Rivers were the main means of communication and transportation between the interior regions and the coastal areas, ultimately becoming important sources of earnings for those who were able to control the rivers.

In the sixteenth century, the Brunei Sultanate devised an administrative system by dividing and allocating its dependencies (*Jajahan*), that were territorially defined, according to the valley of each river (*sungai*) or a major tributary forming the geographical core (Ranjit Singh 2000). The Brunei Sultanate exercised sovereignty over all dependencies, including official appendages and personal hereditary domains. Under official appendages, the highest rank of Brunei state official present was the *Wazir* who would normally collect revenue on behalf of the Sultan. In areas that were held as private property by Brunei nobles, the *Pengiran* and *Wazir* would pay nominal tributes to the Sultan upon the collection of *buis* — the Brunei term for poll tax — and implement policies and edicts they received from the Sultan. Hence, under this system, there were combinations of 'official' administrative governance as well as personal rule that were linked to the power structure of the Brunei Sultanate. Where the *Jajahan* system affected certain pagan communities in some parts of the interior, these peasants were also subject to poll-tax, justice and trade policies imposed by the Brunei authorities.

In the late eighteenth century, the North Western areas of the Brunei *Jajahan* were under threat by the Sulu Sultanate. In the 1780s, the Sulu Sultanate was able to expand its territorial conquest in Borneo through the maritime activities of powerful leaders allied to the Sulu Sultan. Helen Sutherland (1983) had documented that by the mid-seventeenth century, Sulu and Magvindanao attained historical importance as centres for slave raiding and redistribution, preying mainly upon the population from the Visayas, Northern Sulawesi and Eastern Borneo. Aided by the seafaring Illanun (Iranun), Suluk, and Bajau, with the leadership of the powerful Tausug *Datu*, the Sulu Sultanate was able to undermine Brunei's political influence, beginning from Marudu Bay in the north and gradually moving south till Kimanis Bay. The territorial expansion of Sulu over coastal areas, formerly under the Brunei *Jajahan*, encouraged large scale migration of people from the Southern Philippines to set up settlements under Sulu patronage. Some of these maritime traders gradually settled with the local communities in North Borneo.

The activities of piracy, slavery and slave raiding underlining the system of bondage were, however, perceived differently by the Europeans. From the perspective of European trade in the region, the traditional system of 'bondage' associated with slavery and slave raiding became linked to the problem of piracy, which ultimately became a normative pretext for James Brooke to launch 'anti-piracy' campaigns on the local leaders in Sarawak who were allies of the Sulu raiders (Pringle 1974; St. John 1867; Warren 2002). At the local and cultural level, the first British Resident in North Borneo, William Pryer, observed that the slaves were somewhat quite content with their social status as they did not seem to be bothered with 'claiming their freedom' at British ports and were happy enough to go back to their masters in times of difficulty. Pryer described slavery as, "in fact, partaking of the nature of clanship rather than of what is understood as slavery" and how these practices were embedded within the broader structure of the traditional economy and the problems of debt (Pryer 1883, p. 92). Even in death, a slave was bonded to his master, as in how a *Pengiran* related the account of his grandfather's customary burial to Crocker, wherein a slave was starved to death so that he could serve his master in the other world (Crocker 1881). Pryer also highlighted the sacrificial role of the slaves in the event of the death of a leading personage among the head-hunting tribe of the Sundyaks and the Bulungan along the Kinabatangan River (Pryer 1883). In North Borneo, it seemed, slavery and slave-raiding in particular was an issue of security for the commercial interests of the European traders but, apart from colonial documentation on the subject, it remains an interesting topic to be studied — how slavery and bondage shaped social or even political relations and its subsequent demise or maybe revival within indigenous society.

The settlement of the Suluk, Bajau and Illanun in many *Jajahan* areas transformed the political establishments of the affected areas, especially when powerful *Datu* (lords) from the migrant communities began to exert their powers upon the existing *Jajahan* communities. These *Datu* usually came from aristocratic backgrounds and possessed their own powerful political bases, which were scattered over the Sulu Archipelago and the north eastern areas of Sabah. Unlike the Brunei *Jajahan* system, Warren (2002, p. 27) noted that there were more than thirty sultanates in the Mindanao-Sulu region, whereby ethnic groups such as the Tausug, Maguindanao, Iranun-Marano, Samal, and even the Europeans were constantly engaged in political rivalry and territorial conquests. The various leaders of these ethnic groups, such as the *Maharajah*, *Panglima*, and *Datu*, developed their power bases by recruiting more followers, owning more slaves, and acquiring more territories for themselves. Maritime slave trading and ownership by powerful *Datu* provided important revenue and labour resources for the overall social and political development the Sulu Sultanate. Warren argued that the power and prestige of the *nakhodah* or 'trading elites' were conditioned upon the extent to which they could "gain followers and accumulate wealth in the form of slaves, munitions and trade goods" (Warren 2002, p. 167).

The Sulu Sultanate was therefore quite dependent on these *Datu* for the revenue they were generating through slave trading and maritime trade. As a result of the loose network of alliances, these *Datu* tended to be very independent and had their own ways of managing their settlements and political followers. Some of these powerful *Datu* began to invade the Brunei *Jajahan* areas and, in some cases, they were appointed as *Jajahan* head chiefs by independent Brunei overlords. The presence of these *Datu* in the *Jajahan* administrative structure did not contribute to stability under the Brunei-Sulu Sultanates. The administrative obligations embedded within the broader power structure of the Brunei Sultanate were different from the cultural practices of these *Datu*, whose political prowess drew considerably from their maritime trade and slave trafficking activities. Thus, before the arrival of the Company government, the coastal areas of North Borneo were exposed to the influences of the two distinct power structures of the Brunei-Sulu systems. The tendency for both the Brunei and Sulu Sultanates to rely upon local agents — in the form of loyal tribute and alliances — engendered conditions where there was greater scope for *Pengiran*, *Wazir* and *Datu* to conduct their businesses and politics in a more personalized manner.

THE OVERBECK-DENT ASSOCIATION AND THE EARLY RESIDENTS

The mapping of the geopolitics of North Borneo came about as a result of the legal treaty between the Brunei Sultanate, the Sulu Sultanate and Overbeck at the behest of the British Government. What transpired after the cession was the issue of how to exercise control over a diverse population that had experienced varying forms of indirect rule from Brunei and Sulu, on the one hand, and the autonomous pockets of hunter-gatherers and shifting cultivators in the interior, on the other hand. For the Western pioneers, North Borneo was a kind of Hobbesian 'state of nature' where the existence of slavery, headhunting and swidden agriculture underpinned indigenous relations, conflicts and the struggle over natural resources. The greatest challenge for the early colonial powers was therefore to try and persuade the inhabitants of North Borneo to acquiesce to the legitimacy of their rule, and to transform them into loyal 'subjects' who would offer their labour to the new government.

The Overbeck and Dent Association (ODA) came to North Borneo in the late 1870s, when the Brunei-Sulu Sultanates faced political threats from the domestic and international scene.[1] Against this background of political uncertainty, the ODA was able to secure the North Borneo concessions from the Brunei and the Sulu Sultanates. The ODA negotiated the rights to govern North Borneo independently in exchange for annual payments of 15,000 straits dollars to the Brunei Sultan and 5,000 straits dollars to the Sulu Sultan (Tregonning 1965, p. 14). The opportunity for Britain to protect its regional interests as well as expand its territorial jurisdiction was realized when the Brunei and Sulu Sultanates agreed to cede certain territories in return for British protection against other Western imperial forces (Tarling 1978). The Acting Consul-General for Borneo at the time, William Treacher, oversaw the treaty proscribing the sale of the North Borneo lease without the consent of the British Government. This proscription was the main reason leading to the application for a Royal Charter, setting the stage for the establishment of the British North Borneo Company.

The ODA initially employed three pioneering Englishmen to set up a basic system of administration and to make the newly acquired territory safe for commerce. William Pryer was the first Resident of the East Coast, stationed in Sandakan, and the West Coast was administered by William

Pretyman, the Resident at Tempasuk in the north, with H.L. Leicester as an Assistant Resident at Papar in the south. These Residents were required to nurture friendly relations with the local chiefs and to introduce changes with due respect to the existing customs of the indigenous people. On legal matters relating to native customs, these Residents were advised to consult with the local chiefs and land alienation was prohibited unless it was resolved equitably (Tregonning 1954). Cultivating friendly relations with the local chiefs and adjudicating between the legal-rational bases of land alienation, in relation to existing native customs, provided the scope within which the administrative structure took shape.

On the East Coast, Pryer faced the challenge of dealing with headstrong *Datu* who no longer had links with the waning Sulu Sultanate. General lawlessness prevailed on the coastal plains and this was exacerbated by the activities of slave raiders. In cultivating the confidence of the *Datu*, Pryer gave proper recognition to their traditional roles by appointing and delegating government functions to them. A further step in broadening the scope of administration was the inclusion of these *Datu* in dispensing justice in a native court established for petty offences. By incorporating these local chiefs into his administration, Pryer was successful in managing the tense relations among the *Datu* and was therefore able to restore peace in the region (Black 1968).

The administration at Tempasuk on the North West Coast faced similar hostility from the Bajau communities. The collapse of the *Jajahan* system rendered the place unwelcoming, and the presence of Pretyman brought hope to some but also raised suspicions in others. Pretyman had to forge an alliance with those who supported him, whereby he employed inter-ethnic rivalry in strengthening his position. By persuading the Brunei *Pengiran* and the Illanun *Datu* to support Pretyman, it was thought that the Bajau *Datu* would be less likely to oppose the Resident. His efforts opened the way for the wider participation of local chiefs from various ethnic groups in the administration, whereby Pretyman would oblige the presence of a few native chiefs as assistant judges in the administration of justice. Through wider participation, the longstanding hostilities between the Bajau and the Kadazan-Dusun communities gradually died down and trade was resumed through a weekly *tamu*[2] started in the Residency. Despite the confident prediction of one Bajau chief that the Dusun had "never paid, and will never pay taxes" (quoted in Black 1968, p. 179), Pretyman was able to persuade the Dusun to pay taxes, apparently willingly.

Due to his inability to relate to the local chiefs, H.L. Leicester was replaced by A.H. Everett who became the Resident at Papar and oversaw the whole administration of the West Coast, including Tempasuk.[3] Everett also faced the mounting problems of crime and local resistance in Papar but managed to overcome these problems by delegating official duties to the local chiefs under his administration. Local resistance to Everett was slightly more organized than in the other areas because some of the local chiefs were able to procure arms from Labuan. However, their only deterrent was the fear that the British military would retaliate with an even greater force. The fear of British reprisal was the only thing that saved Everett from the fierce local resistance because the reinforcements which he ordered never came.

The waning influence of the Brunei-Sulu Sultanates generated a sense of liberation for some but also posed problems to other local chiefs. Those local chiefs who had the wealth and power to protect their own territories or *tulin* were more likely to survive the disintegration of the Sultanates. However, those local chiefs who only held appointed positions in the *Jajahan* tended to falter in the face of expansionist moves by the independent chiefs or *Datu*. The introduction of a Resident style of administration redefined their roles as powerful local chiefs. By virtue of their positions, they became the first persons to establish official relations with the western Residents. Quite apart from receiving official edicts from their respective Sultanates, these local chiefs now directly interacted with the Resident and, to a considerable extent, actively participated in the running of the administration. The residency system played an important role in starting the process of change from traditional forms of authority to a more rational-legal form of authority that resided at the heart of the Company Government.

In the history of North Borneo, the process of rationalization and the introduction of Company bureaucracy was a product of Western intervention. Weber made the case that in the Western experience of economic modernization, charismatic authority gradually became an unsustainable form of legitimacy and ultimately gave way to the process of rationalization. Changes in the structure of domination from traditional authority to legal authority were inevitable consequences of modernity; as Max Weber noted, in conditions of modernization, "the legitimacy of the authority becomes the legality of the general rule, which is purposely thought out, enacted, and announced with formal correctness" (Weber 1946, p. 299).

The introduction of a Western administrative system marked the emergence of a modern state in North Borneo. Through the ODA, the Company gradually established a Western-style bureaucracy that monopolized the system of taxation, legal enactment, military force and administration to facilitate the economic development of North Borneo. The Company relied on these European Residents to establish social order at local levels. However, these Residents were confronted by varying forms of the traditional structures of authority that had remained persistent under the *Jajahan* system in the West and the *Datu* system in the East coast of Sabah. The *Datu* system seemed to have generated relatively more independent local chiefs compared to the *Jajahan* system, although the latter seemed more stable as an administrative structure. Under the Resident system, these independent chiefs became subject to the assertiveness of these Residents and the Company's administration as a whole tended towards the characteristics of "highly personalized rule with little coordination or centralization" (Ranjit Singh 2000, p. 129).

The highly personalized style of the Residency system was to some extent agreeable with the leadership style of the local chiefs. However, the Residency system was limited to the coastal plains of Sabah and did not extend to the interior regions due to the shortage of staff and the limited resources of the ODA. When the British North Borneo Company finally replaced the ODA, the Residency system was initially maintained but the administrative apparatus was expanded further into the interior region. This expansion demanded for an increase in the number of posts and personnel. The sudden replacement of existing Residents such as Everett by G.L. Davies, for instance, inevitably disrupted the personal relations that had been cultivated and this disruption created suspicions among local chiefs regarding the inconsistent nature of leadership showed by the new administration.

THE BRITISH NORTH BORNEO COMPANY, 1881–1941

> The company, it is true, and the Colony, are only in their infancy, but without any vain boast we may justly claim our part in what has been said of the British as a Nation, and affirm that "wherever we have planted our flag we have introduced law and progress, and have thrown open new fields for the world's enterprise"
>
> Sir Rutherford Alcock, BNBC Chairman, 1883[4]

The Royal Charter was granted in 1881 and the BNBC administered the territory of North Borneo from 1882 until the end of 1941, when the Japanese occupation interrupted Company rule.[5] "Thus armed and authorised, it [BNBC] took over all the rights, territorial and sovereign, conveyed in the original grants of the two Sultans and proceeded as a corporate body, under the Royal Charter, to organise a service for the administration of the territory and the development of its resources."[6] Under the BNBC, North Borneo was administered by a Governor, a nominated Legislative Council and a civil service, with the final seat of authority in the hands of the Court of Directors in London. Galbraith (1965) noted that the Charter was granted upon the condition that the Imperial Government would not incur further financial risks, that the control of North Borneo by a company should present no cost at all to the British taxpayers, and that British trade interests in the Pacific would be secured with the presence of the Royal Navy. The Company became the government of the territory and was required to maintain a civil administration. Under the Charter, the Company was accountable to its shareholders in Britain in promoting the territory as a moneymaking enterprise. The need to protect the financial interests of the shareholders prompted the BNBC to legislate rules and regulations for trade and commerce as the framework for its administration in North Borneo. Attracting foreign capital and keeping a low budget on its administration were the main priorities of the BNBC.

The BNBC operated differently from other chartered companies such as the East India Company, the Royal Niger Company (1886–1900) and British South African Company (1889–1923). For the BNBC, the "overriding question … was how to rule cheaply" (William 1981, p. 3). The first Governor, W. H. Treacher, thus claimed that the development of the territory was best left to private capital, and that the role of the Company was to establish suitable conditions for these enterprises to flourish (Kahin 1947). The BNBC set out to achieve two important objectives. The first objective was the provision of stable conditions agreeable to foreign trade and investments. This involved improving infrastructural facilities, and expanding the administrative framework of the existing Residency system. The second objective pertained to the Company's guidelines on the treatment of the indigenous people in the territory. In principle, the Royal Charter stipulated that the Company was required to protect the property and personal rights of the natives and was prohibited from interfering with local religions and all beliefs. However, in practice, the policy of protecting native property rights was actually secondary to the Company's commitment to protect its private shareholders in Britain.

The Residency system included Assistant Residents and District Officers. However, the administrative structure was quite loose and lacked consideration for the separate roles of the executive and the judicial functions of the administration. These problems were complicated by the prevailing socio-political conditions in the territory, and contributed to the Company's substantial financial drain in the process of acquiring the remaining *tulin* or rivers which were still governed by independent Brunei *Pengiran*. In order to stem further financial losses, Treacher began to alienate large tracts of lands at very low prices in order to attract foreign investors and planters to North Borneo. To facilitate the process of land alienation to foreigners, Treacher began employing a legal-rational framework to secure lands and rivers that were still in the hands of local chiefs. The wholesale commercialization of land did not conform to the traditional norms of some of the local population. The concerns with such practices were articulated by the members of the Native Chiefs' Advisory Council when it was established after the native revolts at the turn of the century.

Financial issues aside, the Company also faced serious labour problems due to the scarce population in North Borneo. The earliest census in 1887 estimated that there were about 150,000 people in North Borneo (Ranjit Singh 2000), but the shortage of labour in the territory was further complicated by the practice of slavery. Slavery was prevalent along the coastal areas of North Borneo, and Pryer related his experience on the difficulty of getting people to work for him. "They offered to work if I would buy them but to work for wages was then looked down upon as much more degrading than being a slave" (quoted in Tregonning 1953, p. 26). The idea of wage labour was still an alien concept in North Borneo and this prompted Treacher to encourage Chinese immigration to overcome the labour shortage in Sabah. In 1891, Treacher declared that "the experience in the Straits Settlements, the Malay Peninsula and Sarawak has shown that the people to cause rapid financial progress in Malayan countries are the hard-working, money-loving Chinese, and these are the peoples whom the Company should lay themselves out to attract to Borneo. Once we get them to voluntarily migrate, the financial success of the Company would, in my opinion, be secured" (quoted in Kahin 1947, p. 57).

Cleary (1996) stated that, whilst indigenous trading of jungle and sea products remained an important source of export value for much of Borneo, the world demand for processed goods in the form of petroleum, timber, rubber and tobacco had increased by the end of the nineteenth century. From 1855 to 1880, jungle and sea products constituted about 44 per cent of Borneo exports whilst manufactured goods increased from 17 per cent to 33 per cent. He argued that the structural changes brought about by the colonial economy were substantial. These included the development of a plantation economy, foreign capital investment in mineral exploitation, and the large-scale importation of Javanese and Chinese workers into the region. However, the indigenous trade in jungle produce remained strong and the established ethnic and geographical structure of the indigenous trade in jungle produce and its lucrative returns could have explained the reason for the lack of native involvement in the plantation estates and mineral exploitation in the colonial economy. Another explanation for their low participation in developing industries and estates under the BNBC was that native workers tended to return twice a year to their villages for the planting and harvesting of the padi crop (North Borneo 1949).

The most disturbing policies associated with these structural changes lay in the introduction of a land coding system and the effects of the commoditization of land upon the lives of the native population. The process of opening up the territory marked the beginning of an intrusion on the livelihoods of the indigenous people. The cultivation of personalized relations between the Residents and the local chiefs were affected by the Company's policies on land tenure, labour and the acquisition of rivers (*tulin*). Cleary (1992) argued that the development of a land coding system for the plantation economy in North Borneo redefined the value of land, which consequently affected native rights to land ownership and distribution. Doolittle (2003) interpreted these changes in land laws as a process of establishing the legitimate authority of the BNBC through imposing the discourse of Western legal-rational knowledge in resource management upon the indigenous society. They both argued that, in practice, the land policies of the BNBC contradicted the legal obligations of the Charter to protect native customs and religious beliefs. Doolittle (2003) highlighted the issue, which divided official opinions, on whether they should allow natives to sell their lands to foreigners at a higher premium, thereby losing potential revenue for the BNBC. There were conflicting views expressed by the officers with regard to the issue of prioritizing native rights to land as opposed to the interests of the shareholders, as well as concerns about natives acting as middlemen for foreigners who tried to avoid paying higher premiums to the Company Government.[7] In fact, the codification of land was a systematic way in which the BNBC gradually acquired monopoly over the natural resources of North Borneo.

The earliest land legislation introduced by Treacher, Proclamation 23 of 1881 and the 1885 Land Proclamation, stated that any form of land transaction between natives and foreigners must be adjudicated and approved by the Company Government (Doolittle 2003). In the beginning, these legislations went unheeded due to the relatively strong presence of the chiefs under the *Jajahan* system in the West coast and the *Datu* system in the East coast. Many chiefs remained relatively independent in areas where the Company's presence was minimal. The BNBC tried to solve these problems by issuing the Village Administration Proclamation of 1891 (amended in 1893) in the hope that it could impose indirect rule upon the existing institutions of indigenous authority in the territory.[8] The proclamation had the effect of legitimizing some local leaders and, at the same time, marginalizing quite a number of independent chiefs who were opposed to the Company's policies.

At the basic or local unit of administration, the Company depended considerably upon the Resident's knowledge of local politics and relations with local chiefs. Due to financial constraints and the lack of legally trained officers, these Residents and Assistant Residents had to run the administration in their respective districts and to resolve issues of legal concern in consultation with local chiefs who pledged their support for the BNBC. At the senior level of administration, the Company's policy on representing the interests of Western investors prevailed. The Consultative Council, set up in 1885, which included the Governor, the Residents, the Heads of Department, and an unofficial member, W. G. Darby, of the China Borneo Company, had the aim of coordinating the activities of the major traders in North Borneo. No attempt was made to encourage native representation, despite instructions from the Court of Directors in London. The new style of administration tended to employ greater emphasis on impersonal rules and the promotion of revenue-earning activities, which consequently undermined the welfare of the native population and brought upon native alienation from the company (Kaur 1998, p. 112). Doolittle (2003) argued that the Company failed to develop an understanding of the local customs with regard to issues of land use, ownership and distribution, and such failure generated a legal-rational bias against the customary ways in which the natives lived off the land. The failure to understand was in some way superseded by the desire to monopolize the natural resources in North Borneo through the legal framework and, in doing so, the BNBC did not appreciate the significance of establishing a dialogue with the existing structure of native authority in North Borneo. This failure brought on widespread resistance from the local population, and that became an important turning point in the establishment of a proper native administration system.

THE NATIVE REBELLION

The degree of native resistance to the BNBC varied depending on the discretion which the Company officers employed in their daily interaction with the communities under their supervision. The crises of personal relations between Company officers and local chiefs began to take its toll as the Company assumed the role of an impersonal government taking control of the natural resources in the territory, which adversely affected the livelihood of the native population. Issues pertaining to land alienation, acquisition of *tulin*, and the collection of poll tax and revenue from jungle produce became contentious as the Company harnessed these revenues to fund its administrative expansion. When the Managing Director of BNBC, William C. Cowie, came to North Borneo on a special mission to deal with Mat Salleh, he expressed his annoyance at how the Brunei Sultan and some *Pengiran* were still holding on to the remaining independent rivers as, "these rivers were ever a source of loss and annoyance to us. Gunpowder, arms, and opium were freely smuggled over boundaries which were never defined and which we could not guard".[9]

The BNBC expanded its territorial influence by setting up more stations along the coastal areas, and by encouraging foreign traders to venture into the interior regions. Under the *Jajahan* system on the West coast, the Brunei Sultan only ceded the areas under his rights to Overbeck. The remaining private *tulin* were still controlled by independent overlords. This prompted Treacher to acquire the remaining *tulin* in order to bring these areas under the jurisdiction of the BNBC. The acquisition of these independent rivers or *tulin* by the Company represented a sense of loss to the communities of these *tulin*. One of the upper river communities of Papar and Putatan reacted by switching their trading activities from the Company-controlled rivers to an independent river in Kawang. The Company responded by forcing the Kawang *tulin* overlord to sell his rights and dispatched a police force to apprehend the leader of the communities that had defied the Company's regulations (Black 1968).

Under the *Datu* system in the East coast, the territories ceded to the ODA by the Sulu Sultanate did not have much effect upon the *Datu* who were independent and powerful as a result of their wealth. One such personality was Pengiran Samah who owned the priceless bird's nest caves at Gomantong, which in the 1880s was producing $25,000 worth of birds' nests annually (Ranjit Singh 2000). Pengiran Samah opposed the Company taking over the caves and refused the official position offered to him. He was then killed because the Company was anxious about the prospect of him instigating a rebellion.

Despite having relative success in establishing some kind of authority along the coastal areas, the BNBC was less influential in the interior regions. The policy of encouraging foreign traders to venture into the interior regions was a way of cutting costs in the process of opening up the territory. The presence of a larger number of traders, especially of Brunei Malays, Chinese and Ibans, began to upset the traditional economic and commercial patterns of the interior communities because their trading practices had caused many natives to fall into indebtedness (Black 1985; Ranjit Singh 2000). Hitherto, the interior tribes, especially the Murut, resisted encroachment from the coastal traders by attacking them or burning the stations set up by the government. However, these traders were now protected by a small unit of Iban police and loyal local chiefs appointed by the Company through the policy of indirect rule. The deployment of punitive expeditions led by the Iban police force dealt a terrible blow to the Murut communities. The punishments were usually quite severe and sometimes a wholesale massacre of a Murut village was carried out by the Iban. Black (1985, p. 48) argues that the lack of proper supervision from the Company Government resulted in the abuse of power by these petty forces in the interior region.

THE MAT SALLEH REVOLT, 1895–1903

Early indigenous resistance to Company rule was quite sporadic and easily defeated by the Company. This changed when local resistance became more extensive and tactical under the Mat Salleh Revolt, and subsequently more violent in the Rundum Rebellion. These two uprisings became the strongest symbols of local opposition to the ways in which the BNBC tried to monopolize natural resources in the territory and undermine traditional bases of authority in the territory. These two events were also important turning points for the Company to establish a more participatory system of native administration.

One of the key figures in these revolts was Mat Salleh who inherited his father's position as a Sulu *Datu* along the Sugut River in 1894. As an independent *Datu*, he continued his father's legacy of regulating trade and protecting the local inhabitants from the exploitative tendencies of foreign traders along the Sugut River. The Company set up its station on Jambongan Island in 1894, whereby it imposed a poll tax and other restrictive policies, creating great dissatisfaction among the local communities and local chiefs in the Sugut area. When Mat Salleh and other local chiefs requested an audience with a representative from the Company in Sandakan, their requests were ignored. Instead of resolving these issues diplomatically, the Company accused Mat Salleh of intending to disturb the peace in Sandakan and sent a strong force to his house in Jambongan, attacking the village and looting his personal belongings (Black 1985). Mat Salleh's escape prompted a $500 bounty for his capture. Displaced from Sugut, Mat Salleh began his eight years of war against the BNBC.

There was a brief period of reprieve when the BNBC sent Cowie to negotiate with Mat Salleh. The first time Cowie met him in person,

Mat Salleh was described as the "Rob Roy of British North Borneo ... the invulnerable ... whose own followers did not exceed twenty, but the Tambunans and others he had picked up on his way to the coast ... all numbered fully three hundred". Before expressing his intention to submit along with the terms of negotiation to the Company Government, Mat Salleh exclaimed that, "[A]t any rate, you will admit that your Company cannot prevent us from dying for what we think are our rights".[10] Mat Salleh made two requests that Cowie immediately rejected. The first one was the release of his friends from prison, and the second one was to be allowed to live in Inanam. Cowie instead lay the terms whereby Mat Salleh should confine himself to the interior of Tambunan and that he would never be allowed to set foot in Sugut and Labuk. The second round of meetings was set for 23 April 1898, where Cowie and Governor Beaufort acted on behalf of the BNBC to grant formal terms of peace to Mat Salleh. Mat Salleh questioned the title of the government to Ulu Sugut and Ulu Inanam, claiming that "they belonged to him and his people, having been made over to them by the Sultans of Sulu and Brunei", a claim which Cowie interpreted as directed against the Sultans of Sulu and Brunei.[11] In less than a month, Cowie received news that Mat Salleh had failed to comply with some of the terms of submission and accused Cowie of not being true to his words. In his diary, Cowie admitted that, "Mat Salleh is right, the terms of submission signed by him were not altogether in accordance with those verbally agreed upon, but the matter can be easily explained and put right".[12]

The basic dynamics of Mat Salleh's rebellion are well documented (Crisswell 1971; Tregonning 1956; Wookey 1956). His attacks covered areas from Sandakan in the East Coast to Gaya Island in the West Coast; however, his last fort was located in the interior region of Tambunan, where he ultimately perished in a shell fire attack in 1900. His campaign was carried on by his followers until 1903, when they finally capitulated. The Mat Salleh Revolt was a costly lesson for the Company and this uprising convinced the government to undertake a consolidation of its administrative system in the territory.

THE RUNDUM REBELLION, 1900–15

At the turn of the century, the new Company Governor, E.W. Birch, abolished the poll tax system and instituted a system of taxation based on modes of production (Ranjit Singh 2000). It was aimed at generating more revenue for the BNBC, discouraging swidden agriculture, and introducing the idea of settlement, particularly to the nomadic natives in the interior. Trading in jungle products used to be prominent among the interior natives but permits were now required to collect and sell jungle produce. In addition, other forms of taxation, through the licensing of fishing boats and land tenure, also became compulsory. Proclamation IX of 1902 became a legal requirement for natives who claimed to own cultivated lands to take out separate land titles for themselves, charged at $2.00 per title with owners made to pay annual quit rent.

The new regulation on land settlement was an important factor leading to the Rundum Rebellion in 1915. Under the new policy, the Survey Department was only able to regulate land reform in the more accessible areas of the West Coast, where the cultivation of wet paddy was extensive and the native population was inclined to settle permanently. However, the policy was resisted in the interior regions of Tambunan, Keningau, Tenom, Rundum and Pensiangan. The native community in these regions were not used to the idea of land being limited, as the Resident of the Interior imposed a three-acre limit on the area of land being cleared by an adult male. The livelihood of the Murut people was gravely affected by the land settlement ruling because they had been the main practitioners of swidden agriculture, and depended considerably on jungle produce to supplement their diet (Brewis 1990).

Most of the Native Chiefs in this region responded negatively to the new regulations on land settlement, and those who opposed it were punished or even imprisoned. Instead of resolving the issue, the BNBC appointed a loyal Muslim chief from a coastal community, by the name of Haji Jamaluddin, as District Chief of Tenom (Ranjit Singh 2000, p. 221). Resistance to the new regulations grew stronger and this inevitably hindered any progress on the registration of titles on land. The other problem related to the issue of land settlement was the construction of bridle paths linking all the BNBC stations in the interior regions. The Murut people in the interior became the target for forced labour in constructing these bridle paths and Harris (1990) contends that this was one of the reasons for them to rebel against the BNBC.

The other two pieces of legislation that were seen as the last straw, causing the Murut in Rundum to revolt, were the tax on native liquor (*tapai)* and the 1913 *Ladang* Ordinance. The BNBC envisaged that through the *tapai* tax, the drinking habits of the non-Muslim natives could be regulated as this would help conserve the supply of rice to the plantation estates and reduce the import of rice. The *Ladang* Ordinance aimed to discourage shifting cultivation in primary forests and to persuade the indigenous communities to practice a settled method of agriculture. The previous system of poll tax under Governor Treacher was less interventionist than the demands of the new regulations imposed by Governor Birch. The policies on the licensing of jungle produce, land settlement, forced labour, and the *tapai* tax had constraining effects not only upon the living patterns of the interior communities but also infringed on their ability to access natural resources for trade and for their own consumption.

The Rundum uprising was led by Antanum, who, according to local oral history, was an influential Murut who claimed to have supernatural powers to bring the dead back to life, restore order in the community, and destroy the BNBC (Black 1985). It was alleged that Antanum was able to stir the imagination of the disenchanted Murut people and received support from chiefs and villagers from around Keningau, Tenom, Pensiangan and Rundum. The Rundum Rebellion was immediately suppressed by the BNBC forces, and fighting between the rebels and the Company's troops resulted in a heavy death toll among the Murut people. After the rebellion, there was a marked decrease of almost twenty per cent in the Murut population from 1921 to 1931, and their numbers never recovered (British North Borneo 1961).

In analysing the Rundum Rebellion, Black ascribed a strong millenarian dimension to the uprising (Black 1981). However, historians are increasingly rejecting the millenarianist explanation, which is often used to paper over events that they are otherwise unable to explain. The problem is both to understand and hopefully to explain why certain figures attract such movements while others do not. Mat Salleh and Antanum were the products of their cultural and social environment but they were also active agents in drawing followers and supporters to help them achieve their personal goals as well as to undermine the legitimacy of the BNBC. It is debatable whether their struggles epitomized the anti-colonial movement in one form or another in the history of North Borneo. But what is certain is that their historical acts were conditioned by some policies of the BNBC that were perceived as oppressive and threatening to their livelihoods. Thus, to understand the Rundum Rebellion and also the Mat Salleh revolt, they must be understood in terms of the already existing patterns of cultural practice, relations of power and traditional authority, to illuminate the reasons for their resistance against the intrusion of Company rule into their lives and their subsequent social disillusion.

THE NATIVE COUNCIL, 1915–35

The native rebellions prompted the Company to make the administration more open to native participation. In 1915, a Government Training School for Sons of Native Chiefs was created especially to impart the elementary skills of administration to its attendees. The first few attendees were almost all Muslims, sons of District Assistants and Native Chiefs. When the training school was closed in 1930, the NCAC demanded a better system of education to be established for the native population. However, education was provided at a minimal level by the BNBC, which devoted only around two per cent of government expenditure ($2,087,617) to education (Kahin 1947, p. 61). The education budget was allocated to supporting eighteen Malay vernacular primary schools and one Chinese school. All the government schools taught in Malay, except for one English primary school in Labuan and one Chinese primary school in Jesselton.

The BNBC played a relatively lesser role in providing education compared to the Christian missions, which became more active in education and medical assistance (Pugh-Kitingan 1989; Rooney 1981). The earliest Catholic mission work was undertaken by the St. Joseph's Foreign Missionary Society in 1859, and soon its establishments were found in Tawau, Labuan, and Tambunan. Other missionaries included the Society for the Propagation of the Gospel, based mainly in Sandakan, the Basel Church — an offshoot of the mission in Kwangtung province, China — stationed in Kudat, the Seventh-Day Adventist, and the Borneo Evangelical Mission, an Australian foundation that worked mainly among the pagan people (British North Borneo 1952). Up to 1931, the main missionary effort was directed at the Chinese but these efforts were extended to the indigenous population in the interior regions, especially after the arrival of the Borneo Evangelical Mission. These churches played important roles in the teaching of English, the development of the Christian faith and, most importantly, the basic provision of health and social services in North Borneo.

The introduction of a modern bureaucracy and wage labour in North Borneo gradually created demands for better education. However, education during the BNBC period was fairly disorganized, and was developed along the lines of ethno-religious distinctions. The Muslims had their own system of reading and writing in Jawi, while the Chinese communities provided their own schools based on China's education curriculum (Kahin 1947). Educational development among the non-Muslim natives, on the other hand, depended largely on the influences of Islam and Christianity through trade contacts and missionary work. Consequently, the BNBC usually preferred to recruit Muslims and, to a lesser extent, Chinese into the civil service because of their high degree of literacy. The recruitment of natives was limited and the highest position that natives filled in the BNBC was the post of Deputy Assistant District Officer.

The Company's preference for Muslims and Chinese in the administration could be explained by the following reasons. The Muslims formed the majority in coastal communities in North Borneo and had established the earliest contacts with Westerners. They were literate, at least in Jawi, which made them relatively more suited for administration than the Kadazan-Dusun and Murut communities in the interior. The traditional leaders of the Brunei *Jajahan*, in particular, were accustomed to holding positions of authority in their respective political establishments and they adapted easily to the new government structure. By contrast, the practice of oral history among the non-Muslim natives in North Borneo did not provide them with the literary skills required for modern administration.

The strengthening of the legalistic function of the Company Administration seemed to evolve into two different structures, involving the segregation of the business interests of foreigners from the welfare concerns of the natives. The Legislative Council aimed to protect the interests of major traders, whereas the Advisory Council for Native Affairs provided a channel for native leaders to voice their socio-economic concerns to the BNBC. The 1912 Legislative Council replaced the Consultative council of 1885 with the aim of developing a better legal framework to regulate the commercial activities of the plantation economy in North Borneo. There were nine official members of the Council, comprising the Governor and all the senior officers of the Company Administration. There were also five unofficial members, including two representatives from the plantation communities of the East and the West Coasts, one from the European and Mercantile community, and two delegates from the Chinese community (Kahin 1947). The Council became a forum for dialogue and negotiation between the business communities and the Governor, with regard to legislation, subject to the approval of the Courts of Directors in London.

As the largest non-native population in North Borneo since 1911 and by virtue of their economic importance, the Chinese were allocated two unofficial seats in the Legislative Council. A Government Secretariat for Chinese Affairs was also specially created to deal with issues related to their working conditions. The Chinese merchants were actively involved in public functions and they usually became the main hosts and sponsors for most government and non-government events (Wong 1998). After the 1915 Rundum Rebellion, Governor Parr created a state-wide Advisory Council for Native Affairs (ACNA) to deal with issues related to the socio-economic welfare of the native population. Although the ACNA had no legislative powers, its creation represented an important step towards the participation of native leaders in discussing issues pertaining to the effects of the BNBC upon the native population.

Native Chiefs and village headmen played significant roles as community leaders among the interior and non-Muslim communities in North Borneo. For the non-Muslim communities, the authority of the village headman (*Orang Tua*) and the village council were maintained for the purpose of resolving issues affecting the communities at the village level. In contrast to the chiefs of the coastal communities, the interior communities usually elected the oldest and/or most respected man in the community to the position of village headman and he was therefore responsible for maintaining social order and social justice in the village community. In return, the services of such persons would be rewarded in kind and they would be given privileged treatment during any celebratory function. If a certain crime was beyond the jurisdiction of the village headman, the case would be referred to a higher council of elders in the village council (Ranjit Singh 1980). Subsequently, the BNBC introduced certain changes to the traditional system by classifying village headmen according to a payment scheme and also making their actions accountable to the European District Officers.

The members of the ACNA included all the Grade I Native Chiefs, and in 1915, there were nine Native Chiefs appointed to the ACNA. Notably, however, there was only one representative from the non-Muslim Kadazan-Dusun community whilst the other eight members were all Muslims. The classification of the Native Chiefs into Grade I and Grade II chiefs was introduced at the turn of the century. The ranking of these traditional leaders became official with the passing of the 1913 Village Administration Ordinance delineating the hierarchy of the Native Chiefs and village headmen. A Native Chief was appointed directly by the Governor, while a headman was a village head appointed by a District Officer with the approval of the Resident. The Native Chief and the village headman became instrumental in dispensing justice within the confines of their administrative districts and villages.

As members of ACNA, these Grade I Native Chiefs played important roles, complementing the judicial system of the BNBC at the village level. The 1913 Village Administration Ordinance led to the integration of the Native Court into the BNBC's judicial system, making the establishment of Native Courts in every district mandatory. The jurisdiction of the Native Court was extended to include arbitration on cases involving the breach of laws and customs of the natives of the District. Native Courts were empowered to impose fines of up to a maximum of 25 straits dollars and imprisonment of up to a maximum of one month. These proceedings were however subject to scrutiny by the District Officer, to whom appeals could be made (Kahin 1947, p. 50). For cases involving the Muslim community, the *Imam* and *Kadi* were appointed as judges for the district, to deal with Islamic law.

The ACNA was rather ineffective until Governor Jardine intervened in 1935, renamed it the Native Chiefs' Advisory Council (NCAC), and restructured its agenda. In the *Memorandum on Indirect Rule and the System of Administration of the Natives of North Borneo*, Governor Jardine proposed the delegation of more powers to Native Chiefs in order to increase their participation in the administration of the state (Ranjit Singh 2000). Governor Jardine wanted to push for greater decentralization in government administration through the NCAC. Two important changes were introduced following this memorandum: firstly, the Native Chiefs would appoint their own chairman; and secondly, European officers, including the Governor, would withdraw from the deliberations of the NCAC (Ranjit Singh 2000, p. 288).

The NCAC possessed no legislative power but became responsible for expressing the major issues affecting the education and socio-economic conditions of the indigenous peoples. Their demands for a better system of education, and especially for English to be taught in vernacular schools, reflected their eagerness to harness their skills for better future prospects. But Jardine was not very sympathetic to their demands. He declared that, "The object of the vernacular schools is not to train Government clerks … the great majority of the boys will go back to the land as cultivators; and it is to train them to be good citizens that the education at the vernacular schools is intended" (quoted in Ranjit Singh 2000, p. 290). Another major issue concerned the increasing economic and territorial encroachments of the Chinese on native lands. The coastal communities were especially concerned about the rate at which land alienation to the Chinese was being carried out by the Company Government and the NCAC demanded an end to this process.

Table 2.1 shows a comparatively higher number of Muslim Native Chiefs than non-Muslims appointed to both the ACNA and the NCAC. Muslims made up about 31.8 per cent of the total population in 1921, 32.1 per cent in 1931, and 34.5 per cent in 1951 respectively (British North Borneo 1952; British North Borneo 1961), but their representation in the councils only once fell below twice this level, in 1935. The higher representation of Muslim leaders in the NCAC added a religious dimension to the functions of the body. The dominance of Muslim natives in the NCAC inevitably laid the grounds for Muslim leaders to press for greater development of Islam in North Borneo. Against the backdrop of strong Christian missionary movements among the Europeans and the Chinese, the Muslims gained

Table 2.1
Membership of the NCAC and ACNA, 1915–38

Year	Muslim	Non-Muslim	Total	% Muslim
1915	8	1	9	88.9%
1916	8	2	10	80.0%
1935	9	5	14	60.0%
1936	14	4	18	77.8%
1937	15	5	20	75.0%
1938	12	4	16	75.0%

Source: Calculated from Ranjit Singh (2000).

greater awareness of their position in society. The Muslim chiefs specifically demanded greater recognition of Islam in the State and also more authority in the enforcement of Islamic laws on Muslim indigenes (Ranjit Singh 2000, p. 293). In 1941, the Muslim members of the NCAC proposed to the government the appointment of a salaried head *Imam* for the territory on an equivalent position to that of the Bishops of the Christian Church; however, this request was turned down by the BNBC.

There were thus two different structures of representation: one involving the mercantile communities and the other one geared towards the native communities. The development of a legal framework designed to protect the mercantile communities was a deliberate policy of the BNBC to attract foreign capital to North Borneo. However, the BNBC's policy of non-interference in local customs and religious beliefs did not work very well with the local population. The acquisition of land, rivers, and jungle produce through these legal frameworks actually restricted the access to natural resources available to the native population. The local customs and religious beliefs of the native communities did not exist independently from their natural environment, and what they understood as their natural rights of access to these resources were now threatened by these legal restrictions. The Company's monopolization of natural resources and their use of law to define access to these resources gradually resulted in the separation of the local population from their natural livelihood. The creation of these representative bodies meant that the natives would have to adapt to these institutional channels to voice their concerns and fight for their rights. Structural distinctions notwithstanding, uneven representation between Muslim and non-Muslim natives within the NCAC remained. This was the overall pattern of ethnic representation during the

Company's Administration, until North Borneo was occupied by the Japanese in the Second World War.

THE JAPANESE OCCUPATION IN NORTH BORNEO

The outbreak of war in Europe and the vulnerability of the Western colonial regimes in Southeast Asia provided Japan with the opportunity to 'dislodge' Western powers from the region, to secure its resources, and to present Japanese leadership as a liberating force to those colonies under Western imperialism (Tarling 2001). The Greater East Asian Co-prosperity Sphere in 1940 was an ideological construct that underlined Japanese propaganda "to foster the increased power of the empire, to cause East Asia to return to its original form of independence and co-operation by shaking off the yoke of Europe and America, and to let its countries and peoples develop their respective abilities in peaceful cooperation and secure livelihood" (quoted in Tarling 2001, p. 128). However, in practice, the ideological rhetoric of liberation by the Japanese turned out to be quite the opposite, particularly in Malaya, Singapore and Borneo.

The presence of a large Chinese community in Southeast Asia posed a challenge to the Japanese military because of their links to resistance movements in mainland China and their deep sense of Chinese nationalism, brought upon by the Sino-Japanese war in 1937. When Japanese forces occupied Malaya and Singapore, Cheah (2003) demonstrated how the extreme use of force by the Japanese military was a ploy to retain social order by expelling anti-Japanese sentiments predominantly among the Chinese. Operation *Sook Ching*[13] was mainly carried out by the *Kempeitai* (Japanese military police) with the aim of suppressing anti-Japanese elements but it soon culminated in the indiscriminate purge of the Chinese community (Cheah 2003). In North Borneo, Wong (2001) argued that the Sino-Japanese war contributed to the politicization of the Chinese community years before the Japanese occupation of the territory in 1941. The Chinese merchant community was actively involved in mobilizing aid efforts by setting up the China Relief Fund in 1937 to aid war victims in China, and in disseminating news about the war in China through the Jesselton Overseas Chinese Daily and Sandakan Overseas Chinese Daily. Wong (2001) had also highlighted the degree to which the everyday civic relations between the Chinese and Japanese communities began to deteriorate as the result of the Sino-Japanese war.

The Japanese Military Administration (JMA) occupied Borneo in 1942 and was based in Kuching. It gradually secured strategic oil resources for its troops and monopolized the trade and export of basic commodities. In wartime, the norms of everyday life were destroyed and widespread hardship among the local population in North Borneo became commonplace. Fujio (2002) argued that, in North Borneo, the Japanese distrust of the Chinese community was such that they displayed similar policing styles to that of the *Kempeitai* forces, who employed strategies of 'elimination' (*Sook Ching*) on suspicious Chinese who were believed to be harbouring anti-Japanese sentiments, particularly those who had been actively involved in the Association for the Relief of Calamity. In order to atone for their anti-Japanese sentiments, the Chinese in North Borneo were required to raise donations for the Japanese Imperial Government. 50 million straits dollars were raised in Malaya, while, in North Borneo, the JMA demanded 3 million. The Chinese were undeniably the most persecuted group by the JMA but wartime priorities for the Japanese troops in North Borneo also resulted in widespread hardship among the natives, due to the shortage of food, high inflation, and the use of forced labour in the construction of roads and airfields. Fujio argued, therefore, that the Double Tenth uprising, led by Albert Kwok, was initially a Chinese-based anti-Japanese guerrilla movement that gradually attracted broader support among the various ethnic communities in North Borneo, including the Dusun, Murut, Suluk and Illanun.

The uprising led by Albert Kwok, however, resulted in a violent backlash from the Japanese regime in the form of a mass execution of sympathizers and supporters of the Kinabalu Guerrilla Force in 1944 (Fujio 2002). It was reported that the war drove many people from the coastal towns to the interior in search of food, as well as to escape from living under the oppressive regime of the Japanese administration (North Borneo 1949). Of the 17,488 Javanese labourers brought in during the Japanese Occupation, only 1,500 survived, due to maltreatment, starvation and harsh working conditions (Fujio 2002).

The extent to which the Japanese Occupation affected ethnic relations in North Borneo remains unexplored. In Malaya, Cheah (2003) attributed the increased mobilization of left wing resistance among the Chinese to the Japanese Occupation. He argued that the discriminatory policies of the Japanese in Malaya had unintended negative effects upon ethnic relations, further entrenching the politics of communalism in the post-war period. He illustrated the extent to which the extreme anti-Chinese policies of the Japanese regime altered their political outlook, forcing them to fight for their adopted country of residence, which inevitably led them to stake a political claim upon Malaya after the war ended. In extending his analysis of the left-wing movement after the Japanese Occupation, Cheah (2006) therefore placed responsibility on the rise of nationalism and communalism in demonizing the politics of the left wing in the post-war political development of Malaya, Singapore and Borneo, particularly in Sarawak.

THE EMERGING CIVIL SERVICE AND THE COLONIAL ADMINISTRATION

The Japanese Occupation left North Borneo in need of serious reconstruction. Civil government resumed after 1946 when North Borneo was administered as a Crown Colony by a Governor, with the assistance of an Advisory Council that was made up of the Chief Secretary, the Attorney-General and the Financial Secretary. The Colonial Government was faced with the huge cost of post-war rebuilding efforts and reconstruction of the colony. From 1948 to 1955, 2.2 million pounds sterling was spent on reconstruction, whereas development expenditure was 3.8 million pounds sterling (Gudgeon 1981, p. 204). Most of the budget was channelled towards the reconstruction of infrastructural facilities and the provision of social services. The BNBC had not put much effort towards improving the health of the inhabitants of the territory, and public utilities were only available in the main administrative towns of Sandakan, Jesselton and Kudat (Baker 1965, p. 80). The Colonial Government, on the other hand, tried to overcome the inadequacies of the previous administration by providing travelling dispensaries, piped water and electricity to all the administrative towns by the late 1950s. There were also positive developments in education under the Colonial Government as steps were taken to provide for the universal education of the population.

Important changes in the administration included a revamp of the Legislative Council, that now differed greatly from the 1912 Legislative Council of the BNBC, whereby native participation in the government was increasingly encouraged. The new Legislative Council consisted of twenty-two members, including four natives, whereas the 1912 Council had no native representation at all (William 1981, p. 19). The official language of the Council was English and, as a result, European and Chinese unofficial members took a more active part in the proceedings than the natives, whose command of the language was quite poor (Baker 1965, p. 42). Under Governor Hone, a process of decentralization in district administration and local government was initiated. The Rural Government Ordinance, enacted in 1951, provided the establishment of local authorities in rural areas, under the supervision of District Officers, with the aim of empowering Native Chiefs and village headmen to control their own finances in rural administration, as well as adjudicate cases related to native customs and Islamic laws (North Borneo 1951). Towards the end of the 1950s, the establishment of local authorities in the West Coast Residency and parts of the East Coast Residency gained considerable momentum.

The Conference of Native Chiefs had been held annually since 1951, aided by the presence of a government officer to record the minutes and decisions made. The Native Chiefs, representing native communities throughout the Colony, discussed problems related to the welfare of the people and used this opportunity to demand greater attention from the government (North Borneo 1960). Under the Colombo Plan, in 1960, and as a direct response to demands from the Native Chiefs, the Colonial Government began to provide English teachers in government primary schools, particularly in the Interior Residency. Overall positive developments in education under the Colonial Government began to materialize as steps were taken to provide for the universal education of the population. In 1952, the first Teachers' Training College was established, and with the formation of the Board of Education in 1956, the planning and development of education became more organized and coordinated.

The transition from the BNBC Administration to a Colonial Government Administration had significant implications upon the evolution of the administrative system in North Borneo. The Colonial Government initiated certain reforms that put greater emphasis on the provision of social services and education, in particular, for the people of North Borneo. These changes were important steps in the process of making the Colonial Administration and, subsequently, the State Government responsible for the welfare of its people and accountable for its actions.

Notes

1 The Brunei Sultanate was facing the expansionist policies of the White Rajah from Sarawak, and the Sulu Sultanate was attacked by the Spanish and Dutch (Black 1983).

2 The *tamu* is a weekly market which provides a formalized means of exchange, and has been popular since the 1860s in western Sabah. These *tamu* became important sites of peace between warring ethnic groups. A stone would be erected and oaths undertaken by the respective chiefs promising to regulate the behaviour of their followers according to certain rules and regulations. The *tamu* is still being practiced in the present day (Ranjit Singh 2000, p. 75).

3 Pretyman left Tempasuk after a couple of years due to ill health, leaving Captain Witti in charge of the local administration in Tempasuk.

4 Sir Rutherford Alcock, Report of the Half Yearly meeting of the Shareholders, speech, 23 June 1883, Borneo Collection, Rhodes House Library, p. 8.

5 The BNBC was finally dissolved in 1953.

6 Views of BNBC with a brief history of the Colony compiled from official records and other sources of information of an authentic nature with trade returns, showing the programme and development of the Chartered Company Territory to the latest date.

7 "It had hitherto been regarded by Land Officers as an accepted state of affairs that any Native of a district, provided he has a few dollars, has the right to select from any vacant land in his district and acquired it on 'Native Title', in other words free from premium, with a permanent rent of 50 cents per acre. An alien applying for the same land pays … an enhanced rent of $2.50 … and a premium of $42.00 per acre." This state of affairs was expressed by Governor Pearson on 13 February (Doolittle 2003).

8 "No headman or chief who has not been expressly authorized to act as a headman under this Proclamation either by warrant from the Governor or by written permit from the chief district officers shall be deemed to have been appointed under this Proclamation or be entitled to exercise any of the powers conferred on headmen by this Proclamation" (Ranjit Singh 2000, p. 159).

9 Personal diaries of W. Cowie, entry for 31 March 1898, Borneo Collection, Rhodes House Library.

10 Ibid., entry for 19 April 1898.

11 Ibid., entry for 19 April 1898.

12 Ibid., entry for 13 May 1898.

13 *Sook Ching* means "purification by elimination" (Cheah 2003, p. 21).

3

CONTESTING THE RULES OF THE GAME, 1963–76

> It is just not true that [Sabahans] feel themselves blood-brothers to the Malays — the marriage would have to be one of convenience, and, if it is to survive, of mutual convenience
>
> Lord Cobbold, Chairman of the Commission of Enquiry for North Borneo and Sarawak, 1962[1]

INTRODUCTION

When Sabah joined Malaysia, it was still a colonial-administered territory. Unlike in Malaya, pre-independence elections had never been instituted and the level of political awareness in Sabah was low. This began to change when the Malaysia plan was proposed in the early 1960s, providing the impetus for the emergence of at least five political organizations defined along ethno-religious lines. The leaders of each political organization, such as Mustapha Harun, Donald Stephens, and G. S. Sundang, emerged as pre-eminent in the local political scene because, as Native Chiefs, they had played a considerable role within local authority establishments in the British Colonial Administration. Prominent Chinese businessmen had also been actively involved in the Legislative council, since the days of the BNBC, as well as in collective organizations through the Chinese Advisory Board during the Colonial Administration. The emergence of a political trend dominated by these personalities was conditioned by their political relations with the

Governor. Because of the relative weakness of political institutions in Sabah, there was more scope for these personalities to dominate the political scene (Loh 1997), giving the appearance that politics in Sabah consisted of little more than their changing political fortunes. The autonomy of these local 'big-men' (cf. Abinales 2000) was, however, circumscribed by the influence of the Federal Government in Kuala Lumpur. The early years of Malaysia were hence a period of some considerable political turbulence, as these local leaders and their associated ethnic elites vied both with the Federal Government and against each other to consolidate the 'rules of the game' in their favour. The diverse ethnic and religious constellation of the state meant that the Sabah Alliance formula, directly imported from the Peninsula, was considerably less stable than its West Malaysian counterpart. Consequently, ethnic and religious politicking — including occasional threats of secessionism — drove the Federal regime to intervene increasingly in Sabah politics. This process reached its denouement in the mid-1970s, when the Federal regime backed the formation of a new multi-ethnic party, BERJAYA, to oust the incumbent USNO State Administration.

REVISITING THE FORMATION OF MALAYSIA

This section re-examines the formation of Malaysia, focusing on the issues relating to the process of Sabah's entry into the Federation. The idea to organize Malaya, Singapore, and the Borneo territories into some form of union had been voiced by the British as early as 1887. However, this suggestion was motivated by the need to protect the future of British interests in the Far East, rather than by any aspiration to encourage self-government in these regions (Ongkili 1985). The idea was again revived when the Prime Minister of the Federation of Malaya, Tunku Abdul Rahman, proposed the political association of these territories in May 1961. The initial response from the Borneo territories was fairly lukewarm (Milne and Ratnam 1974). In particular, Donald Stephens, a prominent Kadazan businessman and newspaper owner, was sceptical of the proposal: "To join Malaya, while we are still colonies, only means we cease to be British colonies and become Malayan colonies … the implication is to hand over to your control" (quoted in Luping 1994, p. 4).

In July 1961, the Malaysian proposal was subjected to debate and discussion at the Commonwealth Parliamentary Association (CPA) with the participation of the leaders of the Borneo territories, Singapore and the Malayan Federation. The CPA discussion was followed by the formation of the Malaysian Solidarity Consultative Committee (MSCC), chaired by Donald Stephens, and joined by the delegations from the respective participants of the Malaysian plan. The MSCC was formed as a result of the general agreement, in principle, among the delegates, that Malaysia was both "necessary and inevitable", and a working committee for the design of the Federation was therefore fundamental (Cobbold Commission 1962, Appendix F). Once these leaders had reached an agreement, an assessment of the opinions of people from North Borneo and Sarawak was conducted by the Cobbold Commission.[2]

Generally, people in Sabah and Sarawak expressed deep concern regarding the speed at which the Federation was to take shape. The estimated population of North Borneo in 1960 was 454,328, and the 1960 census recorded a population of 744,529 in Sarawak. The North Borneo Annual Report states that, "Altogether, over 4000 people from the Borneo territories appeared before the Commission, and 600 letters and memoranda were submitted from the people of North Borneo alone" (North Borneo 1962, p. 3). Bearing in mind that transportation and communication systems in Sarawak and North Borneo were still undeveloped at that time, the extent to which the Commission claimed to be able to collate substantial views from these populations remains arguable and methodologically incomprehensible in the space of a month.[3]

The response to the Malaysia proposal among the North Borneo population differed largely along ethno-religious lines. North Borneo's Colonial Governor noted in his Annual Report in 1961 that "[r]acial harmony in North Borneo has inevitably been subjected to strain by the Malaysia issue, and the new political organizations have tended to divide on a racial basis" (North Borneo 1961, p. 3). The largest non-Muslim native political party, claiming to have about 20,000 members, was the United National Kadazan Organization (UNKO) headed by Donald Stephens. Stephens was the most influential Sabah leader at the time, and most Kadazans accepted him as their *Huguan Siou*, or paramount leader. The party's support for the Malaysia plan was premised on the idea that it would safeguard the interests of the Kadazans against the educationally and economically superior Chinese. The extension of special privileges to the native peoples and the prospect of rapid rural development were given due consideration in an attempt to catch up with the Chinese. The United Sabah National Organization (USNO) was the only Muslim party in Sabah. It claimed to have about 21,000 members, and was led by Tun Mustapha bin Harun. As the Cobbald Commission noted, the Muslim indigenes generally welcomed the Malaysia scheme because Islam was already the national religion of the Malayan Federation and this provided the security which the Muslim leaders in the NCAC had tried to bargain for from the BNBC Government. Both UNKO and USNO were in favour of Malaysia, although they demanded the retention of British officers in North Borneo until suitably qualified natives could take their places in the civil service (Cobbold Commission 1962, pp. 46–47).

The other parties expressed greater reservations regarding the proposal. The National Pasok Momogun Organization (Pasok Momogun) was formed by non-Muslim Dusun and Murut as a splinter group from UNKO. The party had about 10,600 members, led by G.S. Sundang. Pasok Momogun viewed the proposal as hasty and preferred a gradual transition from British colonial administration to self-governance for North Borneo. The reluctance for change reflected the feeling of uneasiness felt by the Murut communities (Cobbold Commission 1962, p. 37). They had been badly treated under BNBC rule, and the memory of the Rundum Rebellion had somehow accentuated their fear of another change in the government. The Democratic Party, the United Party and the Liberal Party were all multiracial organizations, which to a large extent included the substantial number of Sino-Dusun/Natives in North Borneo (whose status remained unclear in the Malaysia plan). These political organizations were led by a motley crew of petty traders, labourers and Chinese businessmen who shared similar views with the Pasok Momogun with regard to self-government in North Borneo. The Chinese were generally less keen on the idea of Federation in view of the prospect of discriminatory policies in citizenship, entry into government service, and their position vis-à-vis the indigenous population (Cobbold Commission 1962, pp. 40–44).

These reservations notwithstanding, the Cobbold Commission concluded that "about one third of the population in both territories [North Borneo and Sarawak] strongly favours the early realization of Malaysia without too much concern about terms and condition. Another third, many of them favourable to the Malaysian projects, ask, with varying degrees of emphasis, for conditions and safeguards varying in nature and extent … The remaining third is divided between those who insist on independence before Malaysia is considered and those who would strongly prefer to see British rule continue for some years to come … There will remain a hard core, vocal and politically active, which will oppose Malaysia on any terms unless it is preceded by independence and self-government: this hard core might amount to near 20 per cent of the population of Sarawak and somewhat less in North Borneo" (Cobbold Commission 1962, p. 50).

Both the British and the Malayan representatives of the Commission unanimously agreed on most of the recommendations except for 'minor divergences' in matters relating to religion, the head of state, the judiciary, public services, the Federal constitution, finance, education and the regionalization of Federal services. 'Borneanization' in the public service was an issue that received the most attention from Lord Cobbold where he personally recommended that, "when expatriate officers are no longer needed for these posts, they should normally be filled by officers from the North Borneo territories" (Cobbold Commission 1962, p. 93). The British and the Malayan members also differed on the issue of the appropriate timing for the administrative arrangements to be restructured under the new Federation. The British members recommended a transitional State Constitution period of a minimum of three years or a maximum of seven years from the date of the creation of the new Federation, to allow for rapid progress towards a full ministerial system of responsible government with a constitutional head of state. This transitional period was recommended as a way of reaching a general agreement regarding the delegation of powers between the Federal Government and the State Governments. The Malayan members objected to the long period of transition and maintained that, "Sarawak and North Borneo should be admitted as States as early as possible within the next twelve months ... A graduated constitutional and legal transfer of powers would only provide an opportunity for protracted delays as a result either of reluctance on the part of the State Government to transfer some of its powers or of the Central Government to assume the necessary responsibilities. The door will then be left open for destructive elements to impede the creation of a strong central authority by exploiting differences among various races and creating frictions between the Central Government and the States" (Cobbold Commission 1962, pp. 81–82).

These two issues were again raised in the summary of recommendations by Lord Cobbold to which he generally agreed with the British members regarding the formation of State Constitutions to prevent any weakening of administrative authority during the transitional period in the Borneo territories. Lord Cobbold underlined further that "Malaysia should be regarded by all concerned as an association of partners, combining in the common interest to create a new nation but retaining their own individualities. If any idea were to take root that Malaysia would involve a "takeover" of the Borneo territories by the Federation of Malaya and the submersion of the individualities of North Borneo and Sarawak, Malaysia would not, in my judgment, be generally acceptable or successful" (Cobbold Commission 1962, p. 94). After the publication of the Cobbold Report, Lord Cobbold wrote a series of letters to the British Prime Minister, Harold Macmillan, Tunku Abdul Rahman, and the Secretary of State for the Colonies, Reginald Maudling, highlighting those issues that had been dropped from the report due to the differing views held by the British and Malayan Commissioners. He was concerned about the pace of the transitional period and suggested that the retention of senior British officers — especially the positions of Governor and Secretary of State — was absolutely crucial, to avoid a sudden breakdown of local administration in the Borneo territories. He concluded that "there is a lot of personal ambition and empire-building in Kuala Lumpur; the Malayans have promised top jobs to several quite unripe Borneo politicians in order to get their support for Malaysia; and last but not least, many of the local head-hunting tribes are backward and fearless and would revert with pleasure to their former pastimes".[4]

THE MALAYSIAN FEDERATION 1963 AND THE SINGAPORE CRISIS

The Report of the Cobbold Commission was an important part of the process by which the agreement to form the Malaysian Federation was reached. It was generally agreed that the transfer of the sovereignty of the three Borneo States to the new Federation would be concluded by 31 August 1963, to be followed by other necessary constitutional arrangements with Singapore and also safeguards for the special interests of North Borneo and Sarawak (Tilman 1963). Official documents from the British records demonstrate Tunku Abdul Rahman's view that the native communities of Borneo would neutralize the Singapore threat to the Malay position, for which he demanded Malaya's union with Borneo even before the inclusion of Singapore (Stockwell 2004, p. ixix). The elite leaders of the Sabah Legislative Council generally welcomed the decided date of 31 August 1963, and were actively involved in the Inter-Governmental Committee (IGC) in preparing the details of the terms of participation and constitutional arrangements safeguarding the special interests of North Borneo. The five political parties (UNKO, USNO, Pasok Momogun, the Democratic Party, and the United Party) submitted the Twenty Points memorandum to the IGC, which became the points of concession to the agreement to become part of the Malaysian Federation. Despite international opposition from the Philippine and Indonesian governments, the Malaysian Federation was officially created on 16 September 1963.

Tilman (1963) identified four issues of political contention that would affect the long-term stability of political relations in the new Federation. These issues included the question of the head of state, the status of Islam, language, and citizenship and migration. These were again raised in the Twenty Points safeguards for North Borneo (later named Sabah under the Twenty Points memorandum), whereby further concerns with the administration were also expressed in the contexts of the civil service and in the fiscal and economic arrangements made. These issues, if not addressed accordingly, could potentially destabilize the relationship between the Federal Government and the new State Government. Means (1968) situated emerging tensions in Federal-State relations within the context of Singapore's expulsion from the Malaysian Federation in 1965 and the increasingly pro-Malay sentiments expressed by Malay politicians in West Malaysia. The growth of pro-Malay sentiments immediately after the formation of the Malaysian Federation prompted the Singapore People's Action Party (PAP) leaders to promote the concept of a 'Malaysian Malaysia': a political campaign calling for equality for all in Malaysia, irrespective of class, colour, or creed. The thrust of the 'Malaysian Malaysia' concept rested on a multi-ethnic society, embodying the "antithesis of a Malay Malaysia, a Chinese Malaysia, a D[a]yak Malaysia, an Indian Malaysia, or Kadazan Malaysia and so on" (Ongkili 1985, p. 190). The campaign was supported by five other opposition parties in Malaysia, which formed the Malaysian Solidarity Convention in May 1965. Ongkili (1985) suggested that the Malaysian Malaysia movement reminded the Malays of the return of the British proposal for a Malayan Union, where everyone would be granted political equality. This challenge was perceived as threatening the constitutional birthright of the Malays, which subsequently led Tunku Abdul Rahman to expel Singapore from the Federation on 9 August 1965.

Singapore's expulsion from the Federation generated political crises both at the Federal and the State level. Some political leaders in Sabah and Sarawak began to call for a referendum to re-examine whether the people in both states were still interested to remain part of Malaysia. Singapore's separation from Malaysia compelled Donald Stephens, and some political leaders in Sarawak, to question the constitutional arrangement for Sabah and Sarawak's participation in the Federation. Some political leaders in Sabah expressed fears that the Federal Government's failure to consult with Sabah and Sarawak on the issue of Singapore's expulsion would engender a greater centralization of power by the Federal Government at the expense of local autonomy (Luping 1994; Ongkili 1985). At the State level, the leaders of the other political parties, namely USNO and SCA, refused to join Stephens on this issue. The general disagreement on the issue to re-examine Sabah's entry into the Federation, within the Sabah Alliance, generated its own tensions in the local politics of Sabah. As the next section demonstrates, the issues that remained most pertinent and sensitive to Sabah gradually became the crucial points for the intervention of the Federal Government. Means (1968) had also argued that the Federal Government found it easy to intervene in local political disputes in Sabah, to tip the balance in favour of those who were more sympathetic to its policies at the national level.

Singapore was accused of trying "to capture the power at the centre" in its demand for greater political equality (PAP chairman, Toh Chin Chye, quoted in Ongkili 1985, p. 182). Kuala Lumpur was determined to remain the centre of power, and decided to put a stop to Singapore's incessant political challenges to Federal authority. Both Sabah and Sarawak objected to Tunku Abdul Rahman's actions resulting in Singapore's expulsion from Malaysia. In the case of Sabah, Federal-State relations were destabilized by the whole episode. What used to be a territory that was politically insulated from outside influence would now be subject to the new rules of the Federal Government.

THE ETHNIC CONFIGURATION OF POLITICS IN SABAH

The ethnic and political incentives behind the formation of Malaysia were quite obvious. For the departing British colonial power, the incorporation of Singapore into Malaysia was desirable, to undermine what they perceived as the growing threat of communism in Singapore. For the Malayan regime, however, any federation with Chinese-dominated Singapore would have to be offset by the inclusion of the indigene-dominated Borneo states. The logic of ethnic representation and Kuala Lumpur's expectation of Sabah as an extension of West Malaysia, however, was confounded when confronted with the ethnic diversity of Sabah's society.

Table 3.1 shows the ethnic distribution of Sabah in the censuses held immediately prior to and after the formation of Malaysia, in 1960 and 1970 respectively. However, the census classifications designed by the British, and

Table 3.1
Ethnic Distribution of Sabah, 1960 and 1970

	1960	1970
Dusun/Kadazan	32.0%	28.2%
Murut	4.9%	4.8%
Bajau	13.1%	11.8%
Malay	—	2.8%
Other Indigenous	17.5%	19.2%
Chinese	23.0%	21.4%
Indonesian	—	6.1%
Others	9.5%	5.7%

Sources: British North Borneo (1961); Sabah (1979).

Table 3.2
Religious Distribution by Ethnic Group, Sabah, 1960

	Christian	Muslim	Other
Dusun/Kadazan	24.9%	6.8%	68.3%
Murut	20.8%	3.1%	76.1%
Bajau	0.0%	99.5%	0.5%
Other Indigenous	2.7%	86.9%	10.4%
Chinese	23.3%	0.5%	76.2%
Others	18.5%	75.6%	5.9%
Total	16.6%	37.9%	45.5%

Sources: British North Borneo (1961); Sabah (1979).

essentially continued after independence, hid a myriad of sub-groups. The constellation of religious and ethnic politics among the indigenous groups in Sabah, particularly in the early decades, is often portrayed as two blocs: the inland Christian groups, dominated by the Kadazan-Dusun and the smaller Murut population, against the coastal Muslim groups, of which the largest was the Bajau (see Table 3.2). The religious data collected in the 1960 census of British North Borneo suggests a more complex picture, however. While the Bajau and 'other' native groups were indeed predominantly Muslim, over two-thirds of the Kadazan-Dusun (then termed the 'Dusun') and Murut practiced neither monotheistic religion; most of them practiced traditional religions. Moreover, even this relatively low rate of Christianity among indigenous groups was a recent phenomenon; in the previous 1951 census, only 8.7 per cent of the population professed Christianity as their religion, and over half of them were Chinese (British North Borneo 1952). As we shall see, religion may have formed a strong basis of support for USNO, but the same could not be said of Christianity vis-à-vis the United National Kadazan Organization (UNKO). Indeed, much of the support for UNKO President Donald Stephens, in particular, came from his position as *Huguan Siou*, or paramount chief, of the Kadazan-Dusun.

The point here is that, as an ethnic coalition, the Sabah Alliance was not as stable as its peninsular counterpart. The major delineation of the West Malaysian Alliance was ethnicity, with religion playing a secondary role; even the opposition *Partai Islam seMalaysia* (PAS, or Pan-Malaysian Islamic Party) was, at that time, more a Malay party than a religious one (Funston 1980). In contrast, the diversity of ethnic groups in Sabah meant that religion, at least for Muslim groups, proved a stronger political bond than ethnicity. With a high proportion of the indigenous population practicing neither Islam nor Christianity well into the Malaysia era, stakes were thus high for conversion.

Under the chief ministership of USNO's Mustapha Harun, and with the tacit support of Kuala Lumpur, the Sabah regime vigorously promoted Islamization and was accused of favouring Muslims in government, notably through the formation of the United Sabah Islam Association (USIA), which Mustapha headed. Under USNO, the Constitution (Amendment) Enactment 1973 amended the Sabah Constitution to make Islam the religion of the State of Sabah (Ahmad Ibrahim 1978). USIA promoted the conversion of Sabahans, but Islamization also came through migration. The USNO years saw major in-migration into the state. Between 1967 and 1976, official net migration into Sabah reached over 85,000, equivalent to almost twenty per cent of the total population in 1960. Approximately half of these migrants were domestic migrants from elsewhere in Malaysia; the bulk of the remainder were Indonesian and Filipino. Much of this migration would have been Muslim; domestic migration was predominantly Malay — Malays constituted only three per cent of the population by 1970 — while the majority of the Filipino migrants came from Muslim Mindanao, especially in the mid-1970s following the outbreak of violence there. Utilizing the extra powers granted him under the 1969 Emergency, Mustapha also began expelling Christian missionaries from the state; over forty were expelled between March and December 1970 (Rooney 1981, p. 214). Sabah's most prominent Christian politician, after Stephens' conversion, Peter Mojuntin, went as far as complaining to Prime Minister Razak about the harassment of Christians under Mustapha.[5]

FEDERAL INTERVENTION, 1963–76

As the anointed leaders of the Muslim and non-Muslim communities respectively, both Mustapha and Stephens had ambitions to lead the new State Administration. But the Federal Government was also keen for Sabah to adopt the same model of ethnic consociationalism as the Alliance Government at the Federal level. A compromise was thus brokered whereby Stephens' United National Kadazan Organization (UNKO, later expanded as the United Pasok Momogun Kadazan Organization, UPKO), Mustapha's United Sabah National Organization (USNO), and the Sabah Chinese Association (SCA) — newly formed from a merger of the Democratic Party and the United Party — formed a coalition, dubbed the Sabah Alliance. The position of Chief Minister was allotted to Stephens; Mustapha was made Head of State.

As Head of State, however, Mustapha continued to involve himself directly in political matters, much to the chagrin of Stephens. The key break came over the appointment of the State Secretary, head of the civil service in Sabah, in late 1964. Mustapha refused to approve the appointment of Stephens' choice, a Kadazan by the name of John Dusing. Stephens accused Mustapha of "meddling" in politics (quoted in Raffaele 1986, p. 144). When Stephens raised the issue with the Prime Minister, however, he received short shrift. Tunku Abdul Rahman said, "Things are done differently in Sabah. There the Head of State is a party man and therefore he is entitled to a say in political matters".[6]

Stephens' position as Chief Minister was, in any case, increasingly a source of concern for the Federal Government, in particular his 'vigorous' support for state autonomy and his promotion of religious and lingustic rights in Sabah (Lim 1997, p. 33). As a Muslim, Mustapha was seen as more conducive to the Federal strategy of "establishing Malay-Muslim hegemony in Sabah" (Loh 1992, p. 228). As the crisis intensified, Stephens was reluctantly persuaded to relinquish the post of Chief Minister to Peter Lo, a Chinese *towkay*, with the offer of the Federal cabinet portfolio of Sabah Affairs and Civil Defence. Even from Kuala Lumpur, however, Stephens continued agitating for greater autonomy for Sabah, particularly in the aftermath of Singapore's expulsion from the Federation in 1965. He resigned from his Federal post over the issue of Singapore's expulsion, after which he returned to Sabah intent on regaining the chief ministership in the upcoming State Assembly elections, which were held in 1967. Mustapha took over the post of Federal Minister for Sabah Affairs in July 1966, after resigning from the position of Head of State in 1965. Becoming a Federal Minister gave him the opportunity to be politically active again in anticipation of the 1967 election. The position of Head of State was filled by Pengiran Haji Ahmad Raffae in 1965.

Although both Stephens' UPKO and Mustapha's USNO were nominally partners in the Sabah Alliance, along with the smaller Sabah Chinese Association (SCA), the two main parties ran candidates against each other in what turned into a bitter political fight. Once again, the Federal Government intervened on Mustapha's behalf through the allocation of a 3.6 million ringgit 'emergency grant' directly to Mustapha, which allowed him to distribute considerable largesse in the run-up to polling (Raffaele 1986, p. 164). As a Federal Minister, Mustapha also had considerable infrastructural support, in terms of the use of official transport, vital for campaigning in as large and rural a state as Sabah. Despite these advantages, the election results were close, with USNO taking fourteen seats (two uncontested) and UPKO taking twelve. The SCA took five seats, with the last seat falling to Yap Pak Leong, an independent candidate who unseated the incumbent Chief Minister, Peter Lo. With enough seats between them to take control of the thirty-two seat assembly, USNO and the SCA formed an administration which completely excluded UPKO and Stephens; Mustapha finally became Chief Minister. Stephens responded along the lines of the dictum 'if you can't beat them, join them'. Recognizing that Federal support for Muslim indigenes had been the crucial element in USNO's victory, Stephens dissolved UPKO and converted to Islam, urging all Kadazans to accept the reality of Malay leadership, stating, "it is well that we realize this and to realize that we must work with them and must accept the fact that if we consider ourselves *bumiputera* then we must also accept their leaders as our national leaders. The Kadazans, in order to be saved, must lose our sense of racialism or rather tribalism and not only accept all *bumiputera* as one but we must learn to feel one (quoted in Luping 1994, p. 240).

The role of the SCA as a political party in facilitating USNO's coming to power is often seen as indicative of a 'kingmaker' role for the Chinese in Sabah; if it had so chosen, an alliance between the SCA and UPKO would also have had just enough seats to form a majority. Whilst there may be a certain truth to this, it is important to recognize the role of the Federal Government in shaping the transformation of Sabah's State administration during the early years of Malaysia. Although it is somewhat counter factual, it may well have been the case that without the financial and logistical support of the Federal Government, USNO would not have won enough seats to form an administration, even with the support of the SCA. What we can say with more certainty is that, in deciding to ally itself with USNO rather than UPKO, the SCA as political party must have been cognizant of the fact that this was where the Federal Government's preferences lay. Allying with USNO may thus have been more a matter of political expediency for the SCA as a political party, in the context of Federal-State relations, than any sign of an independent 'kingmaker' role for the Chinese voters in Sabah.

The improvement in Federal-State relations that followed Mustapha's ascension to the chief ministership was not to last long, however. The riots following the May 1969 election, although not directly affecting Sabah, strengthened Mustapha's position at both the State and Federal levels. At the Federal level, the fact that the USNO-SCA alliance delivered all fourteen Sabah seats was in stark contrast to the faltering support for the peninsular Alliance and lent extra weight to Mustapha's position. This was reflected at the State level, where Mustapha was granted detention-without-trial powers as part of the Emergency. He promptly used these powers to rid himself of political opponents, including the sole remaining opposition member in the State legislature, Yap Pak Leong, who was sent to Kepayan Prison in July 1969, where he remained for thirty months without any charge laid against him.

However, whilst the initial impact of the 1969 crisis was to strengthen Mustapha's hand, the regime transformation at the Federal level heralded the start of a slowly deteriorating relationship between the USNO Administration and Kuala Lumpur. Only months afterwards, Mustapha angered the Federal Government by refusing to allow a British military exercise to take place in Sabah, despite previous agreement from Kuala Lumpur — the first of a series of disputes that ultimately led the new Razak administration to seek ways of removing Mustapha from power in Sabah.[7] Another major issue was Mustapha's continued support for armed rebellion in the Southern Philippines — there were allegations that he actively provided arms — even after Malaysia officially dropped its support for Mindanao independence. But individual issues aside, the increasing discord between Sabah and Kuala Lumpur can best be situated within the broad transformation of the Federal regime following the 1969 riots.

As Gordon Means (1991) observed, when Tun Abdul Razak succeeded Tunku Abdul Rahman as Prime Minister, the Razak Administration was determined to distance itself from the politics of accommodation of the old Alliance. Even before the 13 May incident, certain sections within UMNO had been calling for the party's greater role in government affairs. In Razak's view, the Alliance had allowed too much room for the opposition to mobilize support over 'sensitive issues', to the extent that they were becoming a threat to national unity.

> The lessons of the 13th May tragedy must never be forgotten. Let us not debate and dispute about what started it or how it happened, lest debating and disputing among ourselves, we shall lose sight of the common enemy: namely, those irresponsible elements who sought to sow mistrust and a sense of insecurity among the races and to exploit these sensitivities to their own advantage. These elements created fear and anger by questioning and ridiculing the provisions of the Constitution relating to Bahasa Malaysia and the special position of the Malays.[8]

Razak began to strengthen the economic and political position of the Malays. More importantly, prior to UMNO's General Assembly in 1971, the top leaders in UMNO explicitly supported the move to place the party at the heart of governance; as stated by Deputy Prime Minister Tun Dr Ismail, "we must ensure that every Government policy is determined by the party".[9] Razak decided to set up UMNO boards in all Alliance-controlled states with the purpose of "advising Menteri Besar and Chief Minister on the running of State governments" and to reflect the "government's policy of giving the party a say in the implementation of policy".[10] In order to set up a wider range of support, the less radical opposition parties were invited to join the new coalition. Means (1991) observed that, in this way, the Razak Administration was able to contain public criticism of government policies within the confidential domain of the BN coalition. It was moving away from accommodating the relatively more liberal policies favoured by non-Malays in order to achieve a privileged and protected status for Malays within the context of a national political consensus.

This political consensus was represented by a new coalition called the *Barisan Nasional*. Member parties within the coalition were promised mutual representation in government agencies and patronage in return for political support. It was an ideal set-up for the Federal Government because it could now lay the ground rules for the member parties to 'behave'. By exercising disciplinary powers over the member parties — rewarding loyalists and punishing non-cooperating members — the establishment of the *Barisan Nasional* strengthened the powers of the Federal Government, through UMNO at the core, and gradually diminished the powers of the member parties at the periphery (state level) within the Federation. On the one hand, then, the Federal Government, under the new BN coalition formula, was much more centralized than it was previously. On the other hand, however, Mustapha was increasingly acting in an autarkical and autonomous way, bolstered — ironically enough — by the powers Kuala Lumpur granted him in 1969.

In 1975, Mustapha hardened his stand against Kuala Lumpur mainly due to two issues: firstly, Razak refused to allow Mustapha to seek 100 million ringgit in overseas loans; and secondly, the discovery of oil deposits in Sabah, Sarawak and Terengganu prompted the Federal Government to include oil as a Federal matter. These two issues qualified as both personal and political reasons for Mustapha to review the position of Sabah within Malaysia. In a memorandum circulated by Mustapha on 23 April 1975 entitled *The Future Position of Sabah in Malaysia*, he argued that Sabah would be better off financially as an independent country and also claimed that Sabah would gradually lose its autonomy within the Federation.[11]

The memorandum could have provoked a State of Emergency in Sabah; when the Chief Minister of neighbouring Sarawak had challenged the constitutional framework of the Federation a decade previously, the Federal

Government had declared a State of Emergency in the state in order to oust him. Instead, however, Razak withdrew Mustapha's detention powers, and actively supported the formation of the opposition party, BERJAYA, in August 1975. One possible explanation for this could be that, because of Mustapha's policy of promoting Muslim unity and Islamization, he managed to secure the sympathy of sections within UMNO in West Malaysia.[12] Indeed, for many within UMNO, the prospect of supporting the 'multiracial' BERJAYA against Mustapha's USNO, which had strongly promoted the political position of Muslim *bumiputera*, was anathema to them.[13]

Mustapha's pro-Muslim policies that featured within the political and cultural domains of Sabah's multi-ethnic society had, to a certain extent, realized the vision of the first Prime Minister, Tunku Abdul Rahman, in making Sabah "an extension of West Malaysia" in the pro-Muslim *bumiputera* category. The political partnership between the old Alliance and the Sabah Alliance was a reflection of the friendship between Tunku Abdul Rahman and Mustapha. This partnership was destroyed with the establishment of the *Barisan Nasional* and, instead of working as an equal partner in the new coalition, the Sabah Alliance was relegated to the status of a component party. As a component party in the new coalition, the membership status of the Sabah Alliance became provisional and subject to expulsion. With Mustapha's leadership style being at odds with the Federal leadership, the political position of the Sabah Alliance within the newly established *Barisan Nasional* became increasingly vulnerable.

This vulnerability was exposed when the Sabah Alliance objected to the *Barisan Nasional*'s constitutional amendments in January 1975 that would give the central executive committee greater powers of control (Tilman 1976). Although many critics viewed this as Mustapha's personal grudge against Razak, Herman Luping contended that the USNO Central Committee and the Sabah Alliance Central Executive Committee were genuinely concerned about the *Barisan National*'s attempt to curb State rights and autonomy (Luping 1994, p. 279). It was not unreasonable for the Sabah Alliance to resist the further erosion of Sabah State rights and autonomy. Although the new party system was less tolerant of public criticism, the *Barisan Nasional* did respond to the Alliance's objections. However, a controversy emerged over the membership status of the Sabah Alliance within the *Barisan Nasional* over a period of six months between the Alliance's objections to the amendments and its acceptance of alternative proposals. When the Sabah Alliance threatened to leave the coalition upon the *Barisan Nasional*'s refusal to consider its alternative proposals, BERJAYA took advantage of the situation by claiming that the Sabah Alliance had been expelled from the *Barisan Nasional*, and took this opportunity to apply for admission to the *Barisan Nasional*.

There was no official explanation given for the Sabah Alliance's suspension of membership but the whole situation lent the *Barisan Nasional* the benefit of not doing much in sidelining the Sabah Alliance. The Sabah Alliance's vulnerability was further compounded by Federal support for the BERJAYA party when the *Barisan Nasional* Secretary-General, Ghafar Baba, accepted BERJAYA's application to join the *Barisan Nasional* and revoked the Sabah Alliance's membership within the coalition (Milne 1975). The Sabah Alliance's and, in particular, the USNO party's membership to the *Barisan Nasional* was suspended until a further agreement had been reached, and, in this case, it has been suggested that the conditions for the readmission of the Sabah Alliance to the *Barisan Nasional* were the cause of the official resignation of Mustapha (Milne 1975; Tilman 1976).

Mustapha officially resigned on 31 October 1975 but this did not prevent him from dominating the USNO scene. Hence, a month before his resignation, the Sabah Assembly approved a pension for life for Mustapha, and all the necessary perks to sustain his ostentatious lifestyle. Kuala Lumpur was still wary of his influence because he was still the President of USNO and the Chairman of the Sabah Alliance. The post was then given to his Deputy Chief Minister, Tan Sri Haji Mohammed bin Keruak. Although Mustapha had withdrawn from national politics, the Federal Government was far from being complacent enough to let Mustapha gain any political mileage in local politics.

The Federal Government had to retain a special link with the BERJAYA party because the Sabah Government was controlled by the USNO regime. There was still ambiguity surrounding the membership status of the BERJAYA party within the *Barisan Nasional* because the BERJAYA party was officially an opposition party in Sabah. In order to strategically institute real authority in Sabah, the Federal Government appointed an economist to Sabah's Economic Planning Unit to monitor the State Government's spending, sent out four officers from the National Bureau of Investigation to Kota Kinabalu to investigate timber-rich politicians of both parties, and took over the all-important negotiations that would determine the percentage distribution of Sabah's oil revenue.[14] Although Sabah still retained a degree of autonomy over the control of immigration and the royalties from timber extraction, the real negotiating power lay in the hands of the Federal Government. It was the beginning of Sabah's financial dependency upon the Federal Government and, as a result of the Mustapha episode, Kuala Lumpur was in a better position to institute greater Federal intervention in Sabah.

CONCLUSION

The process of Sabah's entry into the Malaysian Federation had huge implications on political developments in Sabah. The process leading to the Federation was fairly hasty, and Lord Cobbold was particularly anxious about the prospect of immediate transfer of power from the State Government to the Federal Government without due regard for the political maturity and inclination of the people in Sabah and Sarawak. A couple of years after the Federation was concluded, the fear of imagined communal threats again resurfaced in the form of ethnic polarization, galvanized by pro-Malay nationalists, UMNO politicians and the liberal politics of the Singapore leaders. These tensions began to take its toll when Singapore's campaign for a 'Malaysian Malaysia' resulted in its expulsion from Malaysia. The elements of liberal politics tended to generate greater awareness among the Malays of the possible threats to their special position in the new nation. These sentiments had the effect of putting greater pressure on Tunku Abdul Rahman to stabilize the political authority of the Malayan Alliance and to control the forces of dissidence in Sabah and Sarawak. It could be argued that the new rules of the Malaysian Federation were influenced by threats of separatist tendencies, engendered by the Singapore crisis, and similar treatment had to be extended to Sabah, particularly after Stephens tried to call for the re-examination of Sabah's position within Malaysia. In the case of Sabah, Tunku Abdul Rahman capitalized on the internal disputes within the Sabah Alliance to neutralize the key figure that would threaten the Malaysian Federation: Donald Stephens. Consequently, the political marginalization of Donald Stephens and his conversion to Islam represents a symbolic subjugation of the Kadazan political strength — embodied in the concept of the *Huguan Siou* — into accepting the prospect of a Malay-Muslim hegemony.

Tun Mustapha's political rise and demise in Sabah politics was no less linked to Kuala Lumpur's political agenda. Tunku Abdul Rahman's political (and personal) intervention in the Sabah Alliance crisis paved the way for USNO to rule Sabah from 1967–76. Under Mustapha, Sabah became his personal kingdom and his political style soon became too much for the Federal Government to bear. After the ethnic riot in 1969, the regime change at the national level prompted the formation of the *Barisan National* under the new Premier, Tun Abdul Razak. The political status of the Sabah Alliance was demoted from being that of a Malayan Alliance partner to being a lesser party member in the new coalition. As Tun Mustapha faced the diminution of his personal political power, he began to stage his challenge to the Federal Government by threatening to secede from Malaysia. As a way of avoiding a public confrontation against a Muslim leader, Tun Razak began to tacitly support the formation of an alternative multiracial political party in Sabah, the BERJAYA party.

Notes

1. Lord Cobbold to [Secretary of State for the Colonies] Maudling, 9 March 1962, CO 1030/987, no E/1128.
2. The Cobbold Commission composed of Lord Cobbold as the Chairman, two British representatives nominated by the British Government, Sir Anthony Abell and Sir David Watherston, and two Malayan representatives nominated by the Government of the Federation of Malaya, Dato' Wong Pow Nee and Enche Muhammad Ghazali bin Shafie.
3. The Commission arrived in Sarawak on 19 February and reached North Borneo on 25 February, and they made a courtesy call to the Brunei Sultan on 11 March. The Report was signed on 21 June 1962 and published in August 1962.
4. Private and personal letter from Lord Cobbold to Macmillan, explaining the difficulties encountered in writing the report, submission of the Cobbold Report, CO 1030/1028, no. 1.
5. *Far Eastern Economic Review*, 27 February 1971.
6. *Straits Times*, 16 December 1964.
7. *Far Eastern Economic Review*, 8 August 1975.
8. Tun Razak Hussein, parliamentary speech, Dewan Rakyat, 23 February 1971.
9. *Straits Times*, 21 January 1971.
10. Ibid., 28 February 1971.
11. *Far Eastern Economic Review*, 12 March 1976.
12. Ibid., 3 October 1975.
13. Ibid., 16 April 1976.
14. Ibid., 12 March 1976.

4

BERJAYA AND FEDERAL-STATE RELATIONS

INTRODUCTION

This chapter looks at how the 'multiracial' politics of the BERJAYA Government in Sabah took shape within the ambit of the Federal Government's policies, particularly in the 'federalization' of strategic Sabah Government affairs by Kuala Lumpur. The BERJAYA party never really defined what it meant by 'multiracialism'. However, it was a term that was agreed on by both the Federal Government and BERJAYA to politically undermine the pro-Muslim appeal of the USNO party, and as a way of appealing to the non-Muslim electorate in Sabah. As far as the political organization of the BERJAYA party was concerned, a 'multiracial' party suggested a relatively broader ethnic representation within the party and the State Cabinet. The ethnic distribution of BERJAYA's candidates for the 1976 Sabah State election was 24 Muslim *bumiputera*, 14 non-Muslim *bumiputera* and 10 Chinese candidates, as opposed to the majority of Muslim candidates in USNO. Maintaining the ethnic balance within the State Government was important in projecting a 'multiracial' representation. However, BERJAYA's pledge on 'multiracialism' was complicated by the process of 'federalization', here understood as the transfer of certain State jurisdictions on Sabah affairs to Federal Administration. The federalization of a number of State departments and the transfer of Labuan to Federal control in 1984, for instance, did not necessarily strengthen the State Administration in Sabah, but it was an enabling process for the Federal Government to rationalize Federal-State relations, and subsequently the State Government as well.

After the 1969 national emergency, politics at the Federal level was affected by the UMNO party crisis. This crisis was situated in the disagreements between Tunku Abdul Rahman and Razak over the root cause and the subsequent analysis of the 1969 ethnic incident (Khoo 1992). These disagreements led to a split of the party into factions, between those who supported Tunku Abdul Rahman and those who tended to side with Razak. In the previous chapter, I have discussed the emergence of a broader coalition to replace the Alliance, the *Barisan Nasional* (BN), and how it affected power relations within the UMNO party and between the Federal Government in Kuala Lumpur and the State Government in Sabah. The implications of the BN in the context of Sabah politics can be seen in two ways. Firstly, the two main political contenders in Sabah, BERJAYA and USNO had to wage their power struggle within the rules of the BN. Secondly, and more importantly, this power struggle reflected the conflict between the old style of politics and the new technocrats represented in the *Barisan Nasional*, or more precisely in UMNO.

REALIGNING THE POWER STRUGGLE: BERJAYA AND USNO IN THE *BARISAN NASIONAL*

The political dynamics of Federal-State relations rested on the concomitant negotiation of power relations between BERJAYA at the State level and the BN coalition — particularly of UMNO — at the Federal level. Of particular importance here was the conduct and result of elections. Because of the historical quirk that Sabah held its State elections separately from Federal or Parliamentary elections — in contrast to the Peninsular States, which held the two elections concurrently — barely two years passed during the BERJAYA period without Sabah experiencing an election of one form or the other. The following elections took place after BERJAYA won control of the State Assembly in 1976: the 1978 Parliamentary election, the 1981 State election, the 1982 Parliamentary election, and finally the 1985 State election, when BERJAYA lost to PBS.

In the previous chapter, it has been suggested that what prompted the Federal Government to intervene in Sabah politics and force USNO out of power was the ongoing factionalism within the BN, and UMNO in particular, between Tunku Abdul Rahman and his supporters, who generally supported Mustapha and USNO, and those who supported and promoted the formation of BERJAYA as an alternative BN component in the state. In many ways, the alignment of forces within the BN during this period was a strange one: Malaysia's consociationalist supporters of Tunku Abdul

Rahman lined up with the undoubted Muslim chauvinists in USNO against an equally odd pairing of multiracial BERJAYA with the pro-Malay nationalists UMNO.

Personal relationships were important factors here, notably the friendship between Tunku Abdul Rahman and Mustapha. But such friendships cannot be the sole explanation for political alignments; such an 'old friendship' had, after all, existed between the political enemies Mustapha and Stephens. Moreover, to portray the Tunku-Mustapha alliance only in terms of friendship overlooks important reciprocal material benefits in this relationship. For Mustapha, association with Tunku Abdul Rahman remained his best chance at playing a national role — one that he still coveted. For Tunku Abdul Rahman, on the other hand, Mustapha's extraordinary wealth was a key political resource. Thus, for instance, when Razak tried to purchase the controlling shares of *The Star*, in which Tunku Abdul Rahman found expressions for his sometimes critical views of the government, the latter went to Mustapha, who promptly purchased enough shares in the paper in order to block Razak's move (Means 1991, p. 55).

Beyond personal ties, the alignment of the parties was based on competing visions of governance. Whatever its eventual practices turned out to be, which will be discussed further below, the BERJAYA Government had a technocratic, developmentalist vision for Sabah, which coincided with the NEP-driven aspirations of the Razak and, later, Hussein Administrations. UMNO members' wariness of BERJAYA was also compounded by its espousal of 'multiracialism', reminiscent to many of the 'Malaysian Malaysia' issue that resulted in the expulsion of Singapore from the Malaysian Federation in 1965.[1] Tunku Abdul Rahman's faction undoubtedly benefited from reluctance among some UMNO members to the idea of supporting the multiracial BERJAYA party against a Muslim *bumiputera* party, USNO.[2]

Prior to the 1976 State election in Sabah, it was by no means certain that BERJAYA would indeed win control of the State Assembly, even with its strong Federal backing. In its first electoral test, BERJAYA performed badly. In two by-elections prior to the State election, Harris Salleh and Salleh Sulong, both prominent leaders of the BERJAYA party, lost their seats to USNO in Labuan and Lahad Datu respectively. Critical here was the contest for the Muslim votes and the need for USNO to retain the confidence of the Muslim community, to show UMNO that USNO still had the confidence of the Muslim population of Sabah. The Islamic appeal of USNO worked well with the other Islamic component parties in the BN, and the two by-elections were seen as challenging the 'multiracial' concept of the BERJAYA party within the coalition.

As the State election in Sabah grew imminent, the Federal factor on the 'Eastern front' was further complicated by the sudden death of Tun Razak, and the ascension to power of his deputy, Tun Hussein Onn. Lacking a strong power base of his own within UMNO, Hussein's premiership quickly intensified the incipient factionalism within UMNO, as Tunku Abdul Rahman's faction saw his (perceived) weakness as a potential route back to dominance for the party.

During campaigning for the State election, however, Hussein demonstrated his administration's commitment to the political changes initiated by Razak, intervening to prevent members of PAS (Pan-Malaysian Islamic Party), then a BN component party, from campaigning for USNO, resulting in only pro-BERJAYA UMNO members staying in Sabah during the campaign period.[3] Following BERJAYA's narrow victory in that election, further Federal intervention in Sabah involved the systematic restructuring of administrative arrangements between the Federal Government and the State Government in Sabah.

Following the State elections, both the BERJAYA and USNO parties were members of the BN at the Federal level, but at the State level, the USNO party remained in opposition. Whilst solidarity within the BN was expected from both parties, there was no way the two political parties could work together. But neither could the national-level coalition expel USNO that easily, as there remained USNO supporters within UMNO and the coalition more broadly. PAS, for instance, was pro-USNO because of its Islamic predisposition.[4]

Mustapha himself was evidently aware of these tensions within UMNO and sought to capitalize on them as a route back to power in Sabah. He proposed for USNO to merge with UMNO, stating "it is not strange therefore that I propose we accept the principle that we join UMNO in the interest of national unity", and stressed that there was no alternative for the *bumiputera*.[5] Mustapha's move here is reminiscent of Donald Stephens' decision years earlier to dissolve UPKO and convert to Islam (Granville-Edge 2002, pp. 217–40). After UPKO's defeat, Stephens concluded that the Kadazans' (and perhaps also his own) political interests were best served by 'joining' the Muslim *bumiputera* who benefited from Federal patronage; following USNO's defeat, Mustapha similarly sought to throw in his lot with the Federal powers. Mustapha himself had resigned the presidency of USNO, but his successor, Tan Sri Muhammad Said Keruak — widely seen as little more than a willing puppet for Mustapha — continued calling for such a merger through the remainder of the decade.[6] In stressing the need for a strong Muslim-*bumiputera* political front in Sabah, USNO tried to capitalize on its pro-Islamic leanings to convince UMNO to spread to Sabah. USNO was even willing to dissolve itself if UMNO was prepared to accept its members.[7]

USNO's call for UMNO to 'spread its wings' to Sabah did not necessarily undermine its implicit alliance with Tunku Abdul Rahman's faction in UMNO, and Mustapha's presence continued to be felt in the ongoing factionalism within the party, particularly surrounding the Harun Idris affair. In what turned out to be, in many ways, the last hurrah of Tunku Abdul Rahman's faction, Harun played a key role in mounting a leadership challenge to Tun Razak within UMNO in 1975. During his tenure as the *Menteri Besar* of Selangor, Harun's increasing personal wealth attracted the attention of the Anti-Corruption Agency. Due to his popularity among the Malay supporters, Razak offered him a face-saving exit through an ambassadorial post with the United Nations. Harun rejected the offer and he was subsequently taken to court on sixteen counts of corruption. One of the charges involved the *Bank Kerjasama Rakyat* financial scandal, in which Mustapha was also implicated. Harun was also the main organizer for the 1975 Muhammad Ali-Joe Bugner fight in Kuala Lumpur, and Tun Mustapha provided the financial backing of 12 million ringgit through *Bank Kerjasama Rakyat*, a cooperative presided over by Harun.[8]

Despite his ongoing court cases, Harun was elected as one of the UMNO Vice-Presidents at the UMNO General Assembly in June 1975, and was able to mobilize substantial support in his political resistance against Tun Razak and, later, Hussein Onn. When Hussein Onn took over the leadership, he took the opportunity, over Harun's indictment, to expel him from UMNO. This move prompted Tunku Abdul Rahman's supporters in UMNO to lend even stronger support to Harun's political resurrection and his appeals for a remission in his sentence (Means 1991, p. 57). The Harun-Mustapha-Tunku alliance was evident in the light of Hussein's noticeable weaknesses in intra-party manoeuvrings, and the outspoken attacks on the government by Harun's supporters alleging 'communist' influence in the plot against Harun (Crouch 1980). These allegations, however, gradually faded away, and Harun's appeals were rejected and he eventually served his prison sentence. Despite his setbacks, Harun was elected to the UMNO Supreme Council in the 1978 UMNO General Assembly and his nephew, Haji Suhaimi Kamaruddin, was elected President of UMNO Youth.

The BERJAYA-USNO rivalry was embroiled in the UMNO split during this early phase. This split was linked to the faction challenging Hussein Onn's leadership, and became the basis for the UMNO Youth's criticism of the BERJAYA party. BERJAYA was seen as the product of the Razak

Administration and its rejection was related to some UMNO members' hostility to the administration of Tun Razak and later to that of Hussein Onn. The contentious relationship between UMNO Youth and BERJAYA was quite evident during two important events. After less than a year of BERJAYA Administration, UMNO Youth accused the Sabah Government of sacking about 2,000 state employees from various government agencies in Sabah on account of them being Muslims and *bumiputera*.[9] The BERJAYA party was involved in a second controversy when it implicitly backed an independent candidate against the BN-USNO candidate in the Kimanis by-election on 29 January 1977. During the campaign period, BERJAYA Secretary General Tuan Haji Mohd Noor Haji Mansoor publicly declared BERJAYA's "support for the [Prime Minister] Hussein Onn and *Barisan Nasional* but no support for USNO or its candidates".[10] BERJAYA was also accused of openly campaigning for the independent candidate.[11]

The independent candidate, A.K. Aliuddin, won the contest much to the dismay of USNO and UMNO Youth in particular, because UMNO Youth had sent their President, Haji Suhaimi Kamaruddin, to campaign for the USNO candidate, Karim Ghani.[12] The controversy resulted in the rejection of A.K. Aliuddin's application to join BN, and Musa Hitam (then Minister of Primary Industry and a Vice President of UMNO) emphasized that "the independent candidate who won the recent Kimanis by-election would not be accepted by BN through any component party".[13] UMNO Youth did not hesitate to call for the immediate 'dismissal' of BERJAYA's Acting President, Harris Salleh, and its Secretary General, Tuan Haji Mohd Noor Mansoor, from the BN for "challenging the decision of the Chairman of BN".[14]

It was quite apparent in these two events that the factional divisions within UMNO had impacted upon state-level politics in Sabah. The link between the UMNO split and BERJAYA-USNO rivalry demonstrated the importance of the Federal factor in party politics in Sabah. The confrontation between UMNO Youth and BERJAYA was ended in a closed-door negotiation by both sides toward the end of February 1977.[15] The negotiation made BERJAYA realize the political significance of Islam if it was to maintain good relations with the ruling party in BN. Hence, it was no accident when the Secretary General of BERJAYA announced that BERJAYA would look into "formulating the party's constitution based on UMNO's constitution" for the BERJAYA Convention in the coming month.[16] The BERJAYA Government also promised to raise a sum of 10 million ringgit for the proposed UMNO Headquarters Complex on Jalan Tun Dr Ismail in Kuala Lumpur.[17] The BN ploy to keep USNO in the coalition was increasingly evident when BERJAYA could not get rid of USNO, and BERJAYA's 'multiracial' image within the

BN became increasingly untenable when it lost Sandakan to the DAP in the 1978 general election. This prompted Harris to accuse the DAP and USNO of collaborating during the election.[18] During the 1978 general election, the BN had sent ambiguous signals over its support for the competing parties in Sabah, allocating nine seats to BERJAYA, and six to USNO, while leaving BERJAYA and USNO to 'fight it out' via independent candidates for the seat of Kinabatangan — the victor being guaranteed subsequent acceptance into the BN.[19]

In the end, the BERJAYA-backed candidate, Ghani Misbah, won the seat. Kinabalu was the other seat that was won by an independent candidate, Mark Koding, who defeated the USNO candidate, Ghani Gilong, then Federal Works and Utilities Minister. Koding later 'revealed' his support for BERJAYA and applied to join the *Barisan Nasional*.[20] The 1978 general election's results showed that USNO had performed badly, retaining only five seats and losing two seats to independent candidates who were tacitly supported by the BERJAYA party. The BERJAYA party, on the other hand, did very well, except for losing the majority-Chinese constituency of Sandakan to the DAP candidate, Fung Ket Wing. The DAP victory was the first one in Sabah and was all the more embarrassing for the BERJAYA party because the DAP leader, Lim Kit Siang, had been forcibly sent back to Kuala Lumpur when he arrived at Kota Kinabalu airport during the campaign period.[21] More importantly, the victory of DAP, a national opposition party at the state level, showed the ambiguity of the 'multiracial' appeal of the BERJAYA Government among the majority-Chinese electorate in Sandakan.

Despite BERJAYA's apparent victory over USNO, losing the Sandakan Parliamentary seat had exposed the weakness of the BERJAYA Government in dealing with the issues raised by the DAP. These issues included the problems of illegal immigration, corruption, and the allocation of radio and television time for the different languages (Ong 1980). DAP leaders were able to raise issues of genuine social concern that the Sandakan voters were able to identify with. The prevention of top DAP leaders, including Secretary General Lim Kit Siang, from entering Sabah for their election campaign also exemplified the hollowness of BERJAYA's rhetoric of a 'democratic government' in Sabah. The Lim Kit Siang incident was thought to be an important contributing factor to the DAP victory in Sandakan (Ong 1980). The vote for DAP demonstrated three important things. Firstly, it reflected the people's eagerness for greater political democratization in Sabah, which the BERJAYA Government had promised but failed to deliver; secondly, it demonstrated how politics in Sabah was still confined to the selected few, who usually received strong Federal backing; and thirdly, federalization cut both ways for the BN and the national opposition party, DAP. Although Sabah politics became more manageable for the BN, it also presented an opportunity for the Sabah voters to identify with other opposition parties in the Peninsula. But over and above these factors, the DAP victory was a salutary warning to all Sabahan politicians in the BN. Mauzy (1979) argued that the Chinese voters in Sabah were often seen as the 'kingmakers' in contests between Muslim and non-Muslim *bumiputera* parties, as in the 1967 election. However, in the 1967 election, the role of 'kingmaker' rested on the SCA as a political party instead of the individual voter, and its decision to ally with USNO was largely based on the prospects of Federal patronage. The 1978 Parliamentary election, on the other hand, reflected the voting preferences of the people in Sandakan and differed greatly from the political manoeuvrings of the SCA in the 1967 State election. If the DAP were able to capture the loyalties of the Chinese in Sabah, this would have fundamental ramifications for the constellation of BN parties in the state.

If rivalry with USNO characterized the core challenge to the BERJAYA party during its first five years in government, the BERJAYA victory in the 1981 State election constituted the "near annihilation of USNO".[22] This was important, as the rivalry between the parties had been muted in the 1978 Parliamentary elections by the fact that both parties were BN members and thus only able to contest against each other via 'independents'. In the State

Table 4.1
Performance of Major Parties in the Sabah State Elections, 1976 and 1981

	Seats Contested (out of 48)		Seats Won		Seats won as % of seats contested		Seats won as % of all seats	
	1976	1981	1976	1981	1976	1981	1976	1981
BERJAYA	48	48	28	44	58.3%	91.7%	58.3%	91.7%
USNO	40	30	20	3	50.0%	10.0%	41.7%	6.3%
PASOK		26		0		0.0%		0.0%
SCCP		7		1		14.3%		2.1%
DAP		3		0		0.0%		0.0%
SCA	8		0		0.0%		0.0%	
Independents	15	27	0	0	0.0%	0.0%	0.0%	0.0%

Source: Data provided by Election Commission, Sabah.

election, there was no such limitation, and the two parties entered a heated contest in many seats. The results clearly demonstrated BERJAYA's continued popularity over USNO, boosting its share of the poll to more than sixty per cent and winning 44 out of the 48 seats (see Table 4.1). USNO, on the other hand, witnessed the swift destruction of its Muslim power base, even as it tried to reinvent its image by making a 'multiracial' pact with the *Pasok Nunuk Raggang* party, a splinter party from the Kadazan nationalist UPKO party in the 1960s, and the Sabah Chinese Consolidated Party (SCCP), to form the Sabah Front. The Sabah Front managed to win four seats in total, with USNO taking three seats, and the SCCP taking one; Pasok not only failed to win a seat but lost its deposit in over half of the twenty-six seats it contested. The President of USNO, Said Keruak, who himself barely scraped an eighty-nine vote victory in the traditionally strong USNO constituency of Usukan, resigned after the election. The Presidency and the Deputy Presidency of USNO were taken up by Ghani Gilong and Idris Matakim respectively, two erstwhile leaders of the UPKO party (Luping 1994, p. 327). It is worth noting that both Ghani and Idris were ethnic Kadazans who had converted to Islam. This is the first indication — of which more would follow — that USNO was responding to the increasingly complex religion-ethnicity nexus in Sabah by trying to broaden its ethnic appeal while retaining its core emphasis on Islam.

At the national level, the immediate implication of this result was to put the BERJAYA party on the winning side in its power struggle against USNO within the *Barisan Nasional*. Strengthened by the victory of his party, Harris suggested that the *Barisan Nasional* should do away with the loser and let only the winner remain in the coalition.[23] This suggestion was put forward by Harris in view of the impending 1982 general election, and BERJAYA's reluctance to lend its support to USNO — still a member of the BN at the Federal level — if it was selected to contest any Federal seats in Sabah. The existing political arrangement in the BN made it difficult for the BERJAYA party to consolidate its position both on the Federal level and the State. No doubt, Harris' assertiveness was boosted by the turn of events in UMNO, which had seen the core supporters of Tunku Abdul Rahman effectively demolished with the smooth transition to power of the Tunku's arch-critic Mahathir Mohamad at the UMNO Assembly in 1981 and the victory of Mahathir's new protégé, Anwar Ibrahim, over Suhaimi in the UMNO Youth elections a year later.

For the BN, their mission to subdue Mustapha had been successful, but BERJAYA still had to negotiate its relationship with the Federal Government and maintain a strong State Government at the same time. Basically, BERJAYA had to convince UMNO that it had the Islamic credentials to appeal to the Muslim voters in Sabah, and to uphold its pledge of 'multiracialism' in the Sabah Government at the same time. Harris' initial proposal to drop USNO from the coalition was not publicly supported by the BN leadership. The cool reception from the BN leadership demonstrated the reluctance of the BN to lose an alternative that might come in useful, just in case BERJAYA became unmanageable. In fact, the Home Minister, Musa Hitam, rejected the proposal of the Sabah State Assembly to cancel Mustapha's security arrangements and personally ensured that these facilities remained accessible to him.[24] However, this did not deter BERJAYA from devising strategies to eliminate USNO from the BN. Prior to the 1982 general election, the BN Secretary General, Ghafar Baba, issued a warning to component parties, stressing that any member standing against another BN candidate would be expelled.[25] Despite this warning, BERJAYA backed five independent candidates in seats officially allocated to USNO — Kota Belud, Marudu, Hilir Padas, Labuk Sugut and Silam. All the five BERJAYA-backed independents won their seats but were, however, rejected by the BN leadership. As far as UMNO was concerned, as stated by Mahathir, the party was "prepared to take action" on such a disciplinary breach, although no such action was ever taken.[26]

After the unsuccessful bid to influence the BN leadership to oust USNO, BERJAYA had then to eliminate its other political foe, the DAP, from Sabah. In its bid to recapture Sandakan from the DAP in the run-up to the 1982 Parliamentary election, Harris did not hesitate to accuse the Sandakan voters of choosing an 'outsider' and a 'chauvinistic party' to represent their interests in the Parliament.[27] In any event, the DAP won the Sandakan seat with an increased margin — the only loss that BERJAYA endured in the entire state. After the 1982 election, Harris made it his aim to punish the Sandakan voters for what they did. He publicly stated that the BERJAYA Government was a "political government and the approach taken with the development of the State must be political". He was further quoted as commenting that because Sandakan had basic infrastructure, "I don't think you need any other development for Sandakan."[28]

With the shift in political approach, certain changes were implemented to target those who had voted for the DAP. Certain restrictions were imposed with respect to the number of taxi permits and hawkers' licenses being issued. In addition, further increases in rates and licence fees in the Municipal Councils of Kota Kinabalu, Sandakan, Tawau, and Labuan, and in the Lahad Datu District Council were introduced.[29] In what appeared to be a related action, three senior government officers in Sandakan were placed on immediate transfer, and these were the District Officer, the Municipal

Council Chief and another officer in the District Office.[30] Meanwhile, the post of State Assistant Finance Minister was given to a native instead of a Chinese (Ong 1980, p. 166). These controversial measures were apparently Harris' response to the Sandakan voters' rejection of BERJAYA, which indirectly affected a considerable proportion of the Chinese population in the urban areas.

THE IMPACT OF THE MAHATHIR ADMINISTRATION: BERJAYA AND THE NEW POLITICS OF ISLAM

The advent of the Mahathir Administration at the national level prefigured important changes in the administration of Sabah by the BERJAYA Government, particularly in relation to the promotion of Islam. In its struggle to realign itself with UMNO, BERJAYA became increasingly supportive of the Federal vision of nation-building and political integration. As this section will demonstrate, the Federal Government seemed to have its own vision of how Federal-State relations should take shape — a vision that depended on BERJAYA's willingness to accept a more subservient role vis-à-vis the Federal Government. However, a subservient BERJAYA would probably have led to further erosion of the constitutional rights of Sabah.

One of the important elements in the Federal vision of nation-building was the process of streamlining the Sabah State Administration with the Federal Administration. Under the BERJAYA Government, this process of federalization occurred at both the political and administrative levels. Politically, the BN coalition structure in Peninsular Malaysia was replicated in Sabah and was instrumental in asserting party political control over the State Government there. Lim (1997) argued that by extending the party-political hegemony as a strategy of control, there was a gradual loss of state autonomy in Sabah and Sarawak. Comparing Sabah and Sarawak, he suggested that Sarawak was better able to defend its state autonomy than Sabah. He attributed Sabah's relative weakness in defending state autonomy to the existence of intra-party control from Federal UMNO to State UMNO in Sabah. This intra-party control mechanism could be traced from the ways Federal-State relations have developed during the BERJAYA period.

The second tenure of the BERJAYA Government was synonymous with federalization of the administration in Sabah and the growing pace of Islamic reforms in government administration as a whole. Lim (1997) used the term 'Malayanization' to describe the loss of state autonomy as a result of the greater presence of the Federal Government in Sabah and Sarawak, and also the increasingly dominant representation of Malay/Muslim leadership in the political life of the two states, despite Malays not being the largest ethnic group. Under the BERJAYA party, federalization of the various government departments took place under the pretext of nation-building. Quite a number of public utilities departments came under the supervision of the Federal Administration. The authority of the Federal Government was therefore increasingly realized through the control of certain administrative departments in the Sabah State Government.

At the UMNO General Assembly in July 1981, just three months after BERJAYA had won its second term in Sabah, Mahathir replaced Hussein Onn as Party President and Prime Minister, in an uncontested transition. An important aspect of the Mahathir Administration was the growing emphasis on Islam as a strategy of social control and political identification — a means of 'disciplining' the Malays in particular (Mauzy and Milne 1983). The Islamic revivalism of the late 1970s and early 1980s had a huge impact upon Muslims in Malaysia, which led to the rise in *Dakwah* movements calling for greater Islamic credentials in the government, politics, economy and the personal lives of Muslims. In order to overcome the increasing strength of organizations such as ABIM (*Angkatan Belia Islam*, or Islamic Youth Movement of Malaysia), Mahathir wooed its charismatic leader, Anwar Ibrahim, into UMNO with the offer of a Deputy Ministership in the Prime Minister's Department, including responsibility for Islamic Affairs. In 1982, Anwar defeated Suhaimi Kamaruddin to become the new President of UMNO Youth, to consolidate his position within UMNO. Under his leadership, UMNO Youth took up a more definitive role in demanding a greater pace of Islamization and provided a distinctive pro-Malay-Islamic push to government policies. This call for greater Islamic reforms had the possibility of sidelining the political demands of other non-Malay parties in the BN.

The 1983 Constitutional Crisis between Mahathir and the Malay Rulers contributed to the federalization of Islamic affairs that resulted in the Federal Government becoming the final arbiter on many issues that had previously been dealt with at the state level (Means 1991). The Federal Government's decision to rationalize the administration of Islamic affairs was instrumental in strengthening the economic, legal and social needs of the Muslim community through the establishment of the Bank Islam Malaysia, the International Islamic University, Takaful Insurance and other Islamic institutions.[31] These establishments consequently lent the government an effective weapon against accusations that it lacked Islamic credentials. The Mahathir Administration therefore intensified the incorporation of Islamic values into government administration and, in doing so, expanded the role of Islam at the state-level administration.

The consolidation of the Mahathir Administration then saw both a kind of resolution and a kind of intensification of the strange alliances that had emerged between the main Sabah parties and the competing factions within UMNO. On the one hand, the consolidation of the Mahathir Administration saw the fading of the last vestiges of Tunku Abdul Rahman's faction that had lined up with USNO. The victory of Mahathir's new protégé, Anwar, over Harun Idris' nephew, Suhaimi, in the UMNO Youth elections, underlined this. Despite winning a royal pardon for his corruption charges, Harun himself later failed dismally in his comeback attempt to win the Deputy Presidency of UMNO in 1984, garnering barely a handful of votes. Yet, the increasing importance of Islam in the discourse and administration of the Federal Government also intensified the awkwardness of the three-way relationship between UMNO, BERJAYA and USNO. The three-way relationship was a strange one because, under Mahathir's leadership, UMNO's Islamic reforms were forceful, whereas BERJAYA was pulled between the forces of Islamization, to which USNO was inclined to, and the need to keep 'multiracialism' from being undermined by the pressures of Federal policies.

However, in this context, BERJAYA adopted a stance of virtual capitulation to the Federal Government, and to UMNO in particular, ushering in a period in which direct and indirect Federal control over the day-to-day running of the Sabah State Government increased dramatically. The process of federalizing government departments and the overall administrative apparatus of the State Government became an important policy during the second tenure of the BERJAYA Government. The BERJAYA Government publicly stated that it would handover a number of State Government functions and departments to the supervision of the Federal Government as a way of speeding up the process of 'national integration'. Among others, the Federal Government assumed the duties of the licensing of newspapers and printing presses, the registration of vehicles and the management of the Sabah Road Vehicle Department. The Maritime Department, Sabah State Railways, and Sabah Rubber Fund Board were similarly handed over to their Federal counterparts.[32]

In the early 1960s, Stephens had expressed anxieties about the prospect of Malayanization of the Sabah civil service once Sabah joined the Malaysian Federation. The IGC Report recommended as few changes as possible in the administrative arrangement of the Borneo States and even suggested the possibility that certain Federal powers be delegated to the State Governments (Ongkili 1972). Two decades after the formation of Malaysia, however, the BERJAYA Government apparently was facilitating federalization of the state civil service, at the expense of Borneanization. The aim of Borneanization —

one of the assurances given to the Sabah leaders by the Federal Government in the agreement to join the Malaysian Federation — was the replacement of expatriate civil servants by Sabahans once Sabah achieved independence within Malaysia. Initially, this process was hampered by the relatively poor standard of education in the state and the consequent lack of suitable candidates to replace the expatriate officers at the top level of the civil service. In 1960 in North Borneo, there were only 1,280 persons who had completed full secondary education and 1,178 of these were Chinese; while persons having higher tertiary education only numbered 119, of which 115 were Chinese (Milne and Ratnam 1974, p. 43). After joining Malaysia, education in Sabah came under the jurisdiction of the Federal Government. The number of people attending schools had increased but this improvement in educational opportunities had not resulted in an adequate number of *bumiputera* Sabahans to fill the top level appointments in the State Administration.

Table 4.2 shows that, in 1970, the Chinese continued to achieve a higher level of schooling compared to the other ethnic groups. A considerable proportion of the *bumiputera* ethnic groups did not attend any form of schooling, whilst those who managed to achieve the required educational credentials remained in relatively small numbers. The data on the level of schooling shows a grim picture of the pool of skilled workers available in Sabah and it also provides an explanation as to why the *Anak Negeri* (*bumiputera* Sabah) tended to dominate the lower rungs of employment in the civil service, as shown in the graph in Figure 4.1.

Table 4.2
Educational Attainment by Ethnic Group, 1970

	Kadazan Dusun	Murut	Bajau	Malay	Other Indigene	Chinese
No Schooling	70.4%	74.7%	95.0%	43.6%	71.7%	37.8%
Primary	28.8%	25.0%	4.5%	47.6%	27.7%	54.2%
Lower Secondary Certificate	0.5%	0.2%	0.4%	4.6%	0.5%	4.4%
Secondary School Certificate	0.1%	0.0%	0.1%	3.5%	0.1%	2.5%
Higher School Certificate	0.0%	0.0%	0.0%	0.8%	0.0%	1.1%

Source: Calculated from 1970 Population and Housing Census data (Malaysia 1976).

Figure 4.1
Proportion of *Anak Negeri* in New Appointments to the Civil Service, 1975–84

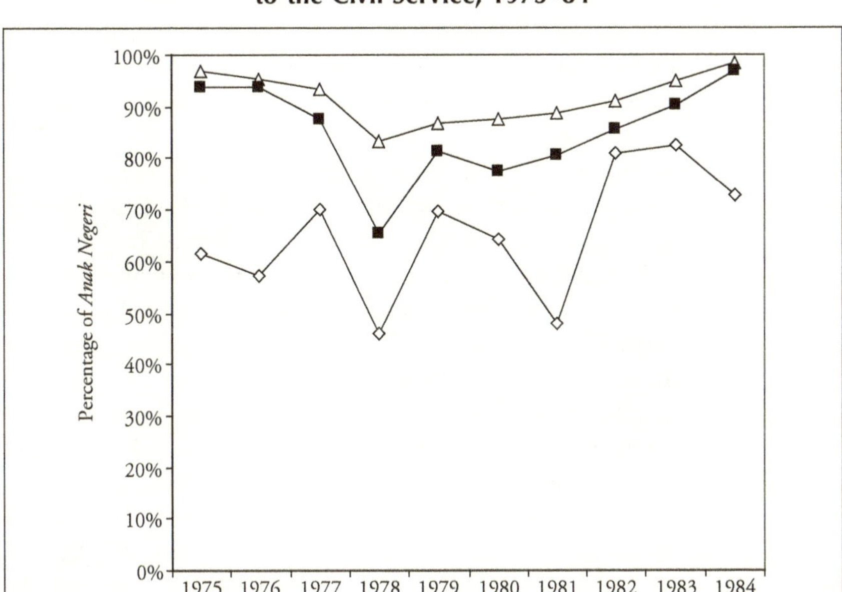

Source: Suruhanjaya Perkhidmatan Awam Negeri Sabah (various years).

The data shows that the Chinese were in a better position to replace the expatriate officers in the government administration of Sabah. However, especially following the New Economic Policy (NEP), the issue of ethnic representation in the civil service was becoming more salient politically. The process of federalization made the rationalization of the Sabah state administrative apparatus more in line with that in the Peninsula. Milne and Ratnam (1974) suggested that the influence of expatriates in Sabah tended to undermine the process of federalization in the state; whilst the IGC prioritized the employment of local Sabahans into the civil service, the Federal posts in Sabah would normally be filled by officers from the Peninsula. Since the provision for the protection of *bumiputera* was also extended to Sabah, it seemed only rational for Federal authorities to send suitably qualified Malays from the Peninsula to secure these top jobs in the Sabah civil service until such time when the Sabah *bumiputera* had the necessary qualifications for these coveted positions. Under these circumstances, there is certain justification to the claim that Borneanization was replaced by Malayanization of the civil service in Sabah. It could be argued therefore that the lack of educational opportunities and BERJAYA's role in speeding up the process of federalization contributed to the failure of Borneanization in the Sabah civil service.

In discussing the rise of Kadazan nationalism in the 1980s, Loh (1992) argued that there was justification for the claim, by the Kadazan leaders, that they had been discriminated against in the civil service. In particular, the domination of the upper echelon of governmental posts by non-Sabahan Muslims contributed to the general dissatisfaction among educated Kadazans. When PBS defeated BERJAYA in the 1985 Sabah State election, one of the first issues that the incoming Chief Minister, Joseph Pairin Kitingan, addressed was the importance of providing the educated and professionally qualified local *bumiputera* with the opportunity to be appointed to key positions within the State civil service (Kitingan 1985).[33] The issue of Borneanization became one of the reasons for the Kadazans' dissatisfaction with BERJAYA, which led to BERJAYA's electoral defeat in 1985. For Pairin and other PBS leaders, BERJAYA's acquiescence to the process of federalization had undermined the principles of self-determination that had defined the terms and conditions of Sabah's entry into the Malaysian Federation. Additionally, Malayanization, through the process of federalization, opened the way for greater Federal control over the resources of Sabah, to which we now turn.

The fiscal aspect of governance is an important issue in assessing the nature of Federal-State relations. Point Eleven of the Twenty Points Memorandum sent to the IGC in 1962 underlined the importance for Sabah to "retain control of its own finance, development and tariff, and the right to work up its own taxation and to raise loans on its own credit" (Luping 1989, p. 13). Sabah's request for financial autonomy rested on three important factors: firstly, Sabah was rich in natural resources and was in a sound position to finance itself; secondly, joining the Federation would not necessarily entail financial or economic benefits to Sabah; and thirdly, Sabah's entry into the Federation was a way of neutralizing the possible threat of communist influence from Chinese-dominated Singapore. The perception that Sabah was "one of the then four partners" in the Malaysian Federation led the Sabah leaders to rationalize that the Sabah State Government possessed legitimate autonomy over its fiscal policies. However, the request for financial autonomy was rejected by the Malayans and Sabah had to concede to the financial arrangement proposed by the Malayans.

Before 1963, the Sabah economy primarily relied on the export of raw materials. Sabah's economy remained largely unchanged despite the increasing pace of industrialization in the Malaysian economy as a whole from 1970 to 1990. Table 4.3 shows Sabah's continued reliance on the extractive industries throughout 1970 and until 1990, and, to a certain extent, justifies the fears of the Sabah leaders that joining the Malaysian Federation would not really guarantee financial or economic benefits to the state. In comparing the pattern of economic growth between Sabah, Sarawak and Peninsular Malaysia, Amarjit Kaur (1998) demonstrated that the economic structure and the pattern of growth that were established early in the century remained unchanged for Sabah and Sarawak, whilst the economic structure in Peninsular Malaysia experienced massive transformation, especially in the manufacturing sector. The lack of a manufacturing industry in Sabah meant that it had to rely heavily on the import of consumer products from Peninsular Malaysia, which ultimately led to a relatively higher cost of living in Sabah than in Peninsular Malaysia. During the BERJAYA period, the price differential between Kota Kinabalu and Kuala Lumpur was 31.4 per cent for the period 1975–80 and 27.3 per cent for the period 1981–86 (Pang 1988, p. 113).

The uneven pace of economic development between Peninsular Malaysia and East Malaysia could have been a major contributing factor to the weakening financial position of Sabah, leading to the loss of financial autonomy for the state. Before oil was discovered in the early 1970s, forestry revenue had been the single most important export income earner for Sabah.

Table 4.3
Gross Domestic Product by Industrial Origin, 1970, 1980 and 1990

	Sabah			Peninsular Malaysia			Malaysia		
	1970	1980	1990	1970	1980	1990	1970	1980	1990
Agriculture, Forestry and Fishing	53%	37%	37%	30%	22%	16%	32%	24%	18%
Mining	—	19%	19%	6%	8%	7%	6%	10%	10%
Manufacturing	3%	3%	8%	14%	22%	30%	12%	20%	27%
Construction	6%	5%	5%	4%	5%	3%	4%	4%	3%
Services	38%	36%	31%	46%	43%	44%	46%	42%	42%
Total	100%	100%	100%	100%	100%	100%	100%	100%	100%

Source: Wee (1995, p. 48).

Table 4.4
Distribution of Major Export Commodities, 1963–86

	1963	1965	1970	1975	1980	1986
Palm Oil	a	1%	4%	16%	4%	6%
Rubber	18%	15%	8%	5%	2%	1%
Cocoa	a	a	1%	2%	2%	9%
Timber	82%	84%	87%	67%	47%	52%
Petroleum Crude	—	—	—	10%	45%	33%
Total	100%	100%	100%	100%	100%	100%

Note: a = less than 1%
Source: Calculated from Pang (1988, p. 105).

Table 4.4 shows that during the period 1963–70, export of timber logs accounted for more than 80 per cent of Sabah's total export commodities. After the discovery of petroleum in the early 1970s, timber and petroleum accounted for more than 80 per cent of the total commodity exports of Sabah (see Table 4.4).

The enactment of the Petroleum Development Act 1974 provided the Malaysian state corporation PETRONAS (*Petroleum Nasional Bhd*) with the ownership and control of petroleum resources in Malaysia. The Act prescribed the distribution of the gross value of petroleum to four parties: the Federal Government receiving a 5 per cent royalty, the producer-companies and PETRONAS taking 41 per cent and 49 per cent of the royalties respectively, and the oil-producing State Governments of Sabah, Sarawak and Terengganu, receiving only a 5 per cent royalty on the gross value of petroleum output (Wee 1995, p. 25).

Largely due to this revenue, during the entire BERJAYA period, Sabah became considerably more important to the Federal financing system. As Table 4.5 shows, there was a net transfer of funds *from* Sabah to the Federal Government between 1976 and 1985, in contrast to the previous and succeeding periods, when Sabah received on aggregate more revenue from the Federal Government than it contributed. In addition, the BERJAYA period also saw Sabah's percentage contribution to total Federal revenue double in comparison to the previous and succeeding periods, irrespective of the amount transferred back. On average, during the BERJAYA period, the Federal Government received seventy per cent more from Sabah *per capita* than the national average; between 1971 and 1975, when USNO formed

Table 4.5
Transfers of Revenue Between Sabah and the Federal Government, 1966–88

	1966–70	1971–75	1976–80	1981–85	1986–88
	Transfers to Sabah from the Federal Government				
A. Federal allocations	299	350	363	1,732	382
B. Federal expenditure	1,140	2,284	3,741	9,283	4,159
C. Total (A+B)	1,439	2,634	4,104	11,015	4,541
	Transfers from Sabah to the Federal Government				
D. Federal revenue	655	1,152	4,922	9,415	2,195
E. Petroleum royalty	—	1	168	496	219
F. Petroleum dividend	—	—	—	932	751
G. Petroleum tax	—	—	845	1,894	1,023
H. Total (D+E+F+G)	655	1,153	5,935	12,737	4,188
I. Net transfer (C–H)	784	1,481	–1,831	–1,722	353
J. Federal revenue from Sabah as % of total federal revenue	7%	6%	13%	14%	6%
K. Sabah population at end of period as % of Malaysian population	6.1%	6.1%	7.6%	8.1%	10.0%
L. Per capita federal revenue from Sabah relative to national average (J/K)	1.15	0.98	1.71	1.73	0.60

Note: Population figure for final period from 1990.
Source: Calculated from Jomo and Wee (2002, p. 38) and *Buku Tahunan Perangkaan Sabah* (various years).

the State Government, the Federal Government had received slightly less than average from Sabah per capita. This shows that BERJAYA was, from a purely economic perspective, in a strong position to make claims upon the Federal Government for greater expenditure in Sabah, especially as Sabah's poverty level had remained considerably higher than national, running at around 33 per cent in 1984, compared with 18 per cent on the Peninsula (Malaysia 1986). This provides further evidence of the *political* subservience of the BERJAYA regime to the Federal-level Government; even when it was in a position to justify strong claims on the Federal Government, it did not do so.

But perhaps the strongest evidence of the relationship between the Federal and State Governments comes from the declaration of Labuan as a Federal Territory in 1984. The proposal to handover Labuan to the Federal Government highlighted the peculiar position of the BERJAYA Government at the time. The Labuan proposal was originally made by Mahathir at a *Barisan Nasional* meeting in 1983. Without further deliberation, Harris subsequently obtained the Sabah Cabinet's approval (Means 1991). The proposal was described as the "prize winning bombshell" of all the bombshells dropped by the BERJAYA government.[34] No referendum was conducted on the proposal and, in his defence, Harris stressed that "we are not giving away our territory because the Federal Government was in a position to develop the island".[35] However, subsequent events raised questions related to the real bargain for the unprecedented cession of Labuan. On 24 August 1983, the *Daily Express* reported that Mustapha, who had been reinstated as USNO president, urged the USNO division in Labuan to oppose the move and hold a public demonstration against it.

In February 1984, Mahathir proposed the expulsion of USNO from the *Barisan Nasional*.[36] On 21 February 1984, the Labuan USNO division unanimously voted to dissolve itself after twenty years of existence, in a show of support for the move to make Labuan a Federal Territory. Encik Mohd Omar Bledram, USNO's Divisional Head in Labuan, announced the dissolution of all twenty-seven branches with 4,563 members.[37] The next day, the USNO headquarters in Kota Kinabalu claimed that the dissolution of Labuan USNO was invalid as the meeting was only attended by ten people.[38] However, USNO began to crumble as its members heeded the advice of the Prime Minister that "those who cherish the principles of *Barisan Nasional* should leave the party as it was no longer of any use".[39] Even if USNO officially denied that it had sought to campaign against the declaration of Labuan as a Federal Territory, its fate was sealed once Mahathir had made his official statement. On 27 February 1984, the UMNO Supreme Council unanimously voted that USNO should be expelled from the *Barisan Nasional*.[40]

The expulsion of USNO from the *Barisan Nasional* became official on 15 April 1984, one day before Labuan became Federal Territory. Mahathir justified the expulsion by declaring that USNO had "stabbed the government in the back" by its move against the Constitutional Amendment issue and the decision to turn Labuan into a Federal Territory.[41] Harris commented that fifteen had been an auspicious number for BERJAYA because BERJAYA was formed on 15 July 1975, BERJAYA had won the Sabah State election against USNO on 15 April 1976, and, finally, the *Barisan Nasional* expelled USNO on 15 April 1984.[42] In an unprecedented turn of events, the *Barisan Nasional* also accepted into its fold the five independent candidates who had stood against USNO-BN candidates in the 1982 general elections and had won with strong BERJAYA machinery behind them.[43] The five candidates were initially rejected by Mahathir in the 1982 general elections on the grounds that BERJAYA had breached *Barisan Nasional* rules.

As Gordon Means (1991, p. 159) noted, "for many Sabahans, the transfer of Labuan to Federal control confirmed the view that the BERJAYA government was dependent on Federal support and its inability to withstand any pressure from Kuala Lumpur, therefore affirming the accusation that it failed to defend Sabah State interests". However, the events that built up towards the expulsion of USNO from the *Barisan Nasional* also begged the question of whether the Federal Territory move on Labuan was linked to Harris' proposal, after BERJAYA's landslide victory in the 1981 Sabah State election, that USNO should be dropped from the *Barisan Nasional.* The unprecedented change of political stance on the part of the BN leadership seemed to imply that the price for USNO's expulsion and the acceptance of five independent candidates into BN came in the form of Federal control over Labuan. Unlike Selangor, when Kuala Lumpur was ceded to federal control, Sabah did not receive any financial compensation for ceding Labuan to the Federal Government; instead, State Finance Minister Mohd. Noor Mansoor reassured that the 'compensation' for the Labuan Federal Territory Bill would be "real integration" between the Federal Government and the State Government in Sabah.[44]

In retrospect, Harris expressed a sense of regret when he compared the handing over of Labuan to Kuala Lumpur to that of a son's unrequited affection for the father. His only regret was that the Federal Government never really developed Labuan properly. Harris expected the Federal Government, as *bapa* (father), to treat Labuan as an *anak* (child). However, he was disillusioned by the Federal Government's letdown and, in his own words, said that the whole process was like "bapa kasi makan ikan masin" (meaning 'the father neglecting the child'). When asked about the success of the BERJAYA Government in managing the crises of Federal-State relations, Harris was less inclined to claim the party's pro-Federal stance. Instead, he claimed that USNO was more supportive of the Federal Government, whereas the priorities of the BERJAYA Government's policies were aimed at achieving national integration in the interest of the Sabah people.[45]

CONCLUSION

The role 'federalization' in the discourse and political practices of the BERJAYA Government reflected the process of the realignment of political forces in the Peninsula, which continued to dominate Sabahan politics even after BERJAYA's success in the 1976 State election, as contending factions on both sides of Malaysia lined up over issues such as Harun Idris' position. Hopes within BERJAYA that the Federal-based BN would side unambiguously with BERJAYA, to replace USNO as the main coalition partner in the State, continued to be frustrated as USNO continued to be allotted coalition seats in the Federal elections of 1978 and 1982.

In addition, this period saw the increasing role of the Federal Government in the administration of the State. The BERJAYA Administration handed over the control of a number of Sabah government departments and statutory bodies to the Federal Government in the name of 'national integration'. In addition to the laudable goal of promoting national unity, however, such moves by the BERJAYA Government may have been motivated by a desire to win favour in its continuing confrontation with USNO at the State level. Moreover, when BERJAYA agreed to cede control of the island of Labuan to the Federal Government, the latter's ambiguity towards the political situation in Sabah was finally resolved, and coalition support for USNO was unceremoniously cut. Whilst the machinations of Federal-State relations were clearly important during the BERJAYA period, they alone cannot account for the trajectory of Sabah politics during this period. At the State level, it was the politics and discourse of development that formed the major division between the contending parties.

Notes

1 *Far Eastern Economic Review*, 16 April 1976.
2 Ibid., 3 October 1975.
3 Ibid., 7 April 1975.
4 Ibid., 2 September 1977.
5 Ibid., 12 July 1976.
6 *Daily Express*, 27 June 1979.
7 Ibid., 15 June 1979.
8 *Far Eastern Economic Review*, 25 July 1975.
9 *Daily Express*, 3 February 1977.
10 Ibid., 28 January 1977.
11 Ibid., 17 February 1977.
12 *Far Eastern Economic Review*, 2 September 1977.

[13] *Daily Express*, 4 February 1977.
[14] Ibid., 5 February 1977.
[15] Ibid., 24 February 1977
[16] Ibid., 7 February 1977.
[17] Ibid., 26 June 1977.
[18] Ibid., 3 April 1982.
[19] Ibid., 26 June 1978.
[20] *Far Eastern Economic Review*, 28 July 1978.
[21] Ibid., 28 July 1978.
[22] Ibid., 23 April 1981.
[23] Ibid., 23 April 1981.
[24] Ibid., 11 December 1981.
[25] *Daily Express*, 13 April 1982.
[26] Ibid., 30 April 1982
[27] Ibid., 3 April 1982.
[28] Ibid., 7 May 1982
[29] Ibid., 20 April 1982
[30] *Far Eastern Economic Review*, 13 May 1982.
[31] This will be further discussed in Chapter 6 under *Dakwah Islamiah*.
[32] *Daily Express*, 18 May 1983.
[33] "Sekarang semakin ramai anak-anak tempatan mempunyai tenaga professional dan mahir. Oleh yang demikian, tidak ada sebabnya mereka tidak diberikan peluang bagi menyumbangkan tenaga professional dan kemahiran mereka bagi membangunkan negeri ini, ... jika ada pegawai-pegawai kontrak luar tidak lagi disambung kontrak mereka, tidak bererti mereka dipecat, tetapi bersesuaian dengan syarat-syarat kontrak".
[34] *Daily Express*, 13 August 1983.
[35] Ibid., 22 August 1983.
[36] Ibid., 20 April 1984.
[37] Ibid., 22 February 1984.
[38] Ibid., 23 February 1984.
[39] Ibid., 24 February 1984.
[40] Ibid., 25 February 1984; Ibid., 27 February 1984.
[41] Ibid., 14 April 1984.
[42] Ibid., 19 April 1984.
[43] Ibid., 16 April 1984. The five candidates were Yusoff Yakub (Hilir Padas), Haji Affendi Stephen (Marudu), Haji Yahya Lampong (Kota Belud), Abdilah Hassan (Semporna), and Hassan Sandukong (Labuk Sugut).
[44] Ibid., 9 April 1984.
[45] Harris Salleh, interview by the author, Balung, April 2003.

5

DEVELOPMENT AND PATRONAGE

INTRODUCTION

Under BERJAYA, the discourse of development was used as a strategy for political support. In analysing the 1994 Sabah State election, Loh (1997) contended that the issue of development became central to the campaign tactics of the BN during the Mahathir Administration. The discourse of development was employed as a way to convince the Sabah electorate that the opposition government in Sabah, the PBS (*Parti Bersatu Sabah*, or Sabah United Party), had failed to bring progress and development to Sabah. The BN also introduced the slogan *Sabah Baru* (New Sabah) to denote a new image of Sabah as a developed state under the care of BN. Under the rhetoric of *Sabah Baru*, the BN pledged to build a university in Sabah, improve the education system, create low-cost housing, expand rural development programmes, and industrialize the Sabah economy. The 'developmentalist' approach or 'politics of development' was employed again in the 1999 Sabah State election, together with the successful manipulation of the '3Ms': money politics, the BN electoral machine and the media (Loh 2003). The long list of development plans — forty-four of them published in the local newspaper in twelve days, from 28 February 1999 to 11 March 1999 — also contributed to the BN's success in the election (Loh 2003).

If the 1990s saw 'development' discourse in Sabah reach its apogee, it was under BERJAYA that Sabah began to experience the politicization of development on a broader scale. Long before the BN was promising a New [developed] Sabah if the PBS was ousted, Harris had made explicit the link between support for BERJAYA and the benefits of development. After the DAP won the Sandakan Federal constituency during the 1978 Federal election, Harris announced that "the Party BERJAYA's politics was the politics of development".[1] When the Sandakan electorate voted again for the DAP in the 1982 Federal election, Harris declared to the voters that there would be no development in Sandakan.[2] Other areas known for supporting the opposition also received similar warnings. "If the people still want USNO to represent them in Banggi, Semporna, and Kota Belud", Harris declared, "we will not visit these areas and development and progress will suffer".[3] In the final dramatic years of BERJAYA's rule, Harris finally practiced his political mantra by revoking the district status of Tambunan after Pairin was re-elected as its representative following his expulsion from BERJAYA.

In tracing the emergence of this particular type of developmentalist approach of the BERJAYA Administration, it is important to understand how BERJAYA employed the ideology of development in mobilizing support for its party. The main economic pillars of the NEP involved the modernization of rural life, and this was to be achieved through the "elimination of poverty" and the "restructuring of the economy regardless of ethnicity" (Malaysia 1971, p. 1). The high incidence of poverty in Sabah prompted BERJAYA to make rural development an important priority in its economic agenda. The allocation of timber licences and the economic expansion of the Sabah Foundation provided the necessary capital for BERJAYA to fund the creation of various cooperative agencies as the economic strategy for rural development. These cooperative agencies aimed to provide an important production and marketing network for small-scale agriculture and farming in the rural areas. In providing social development in the rural areas, the BERJAYA Government initiated certain reforms within the Village Development Committees (JKK, Jawatan Kuasa Kemajuan Kampung) to improve the delivery mechanism of government development packages to the rural areas. However, the existence of several opposition strongholds made the BERJAYA Government selective in their implementation of development policies, consequently giving rise to a situation where development became highly politicized through patronage.

ECONOMIC TRANSFORMATION UNDER BERJAYA

When BERJAYA took over the administration of Sabah, the economy apparently had high potential but also massive problems. At independence, the State's vast timber reserves had been seen as the key exploitable resource, but the formation of Malaysia was also expected to bring more industrial development to Sabah (Kaur 1998). The discovery of oil in the early 1970s had added to the State's exploitable primary reserves. In 1975, the per capita gross domestic product (GDP) of the State was ten per cent higher than the national average, although this would have been counterbalanced to some degree by the higher prices in the State (Jomo and Wee 2002). Yet poverty rates in the State were also among the highest in Malaysia, standing at 51.7 per cent of households when the first data was produced in 1976 — far above the national rate of 37.7 per cent, although still lower than the rate in the northern Malay states of the Peninsula (Malaysia 1986; Malaysia 1991). In addition, the flipside of the State's rich resource endowment was a very low industrialization rate. The secondary sector — manufacturing and construction — contributed less than 10 per cent of State GDP. In comparison, the contribution of this sector to the Malaysian economy as a whole was almost double, at 19.0 per cent (Ibid.).

In 1983, as BERJAYA neared the end of what was to be its last term in power, the office of the Chief Minister claimed that "the achievements of the BERJAYA government in accelerating socio-economic development and in raising living standards and the quality of life of the people of Sabah in the

Figure 5.1
Paved and Gravel Road Mileage in Sabah, 1967–85

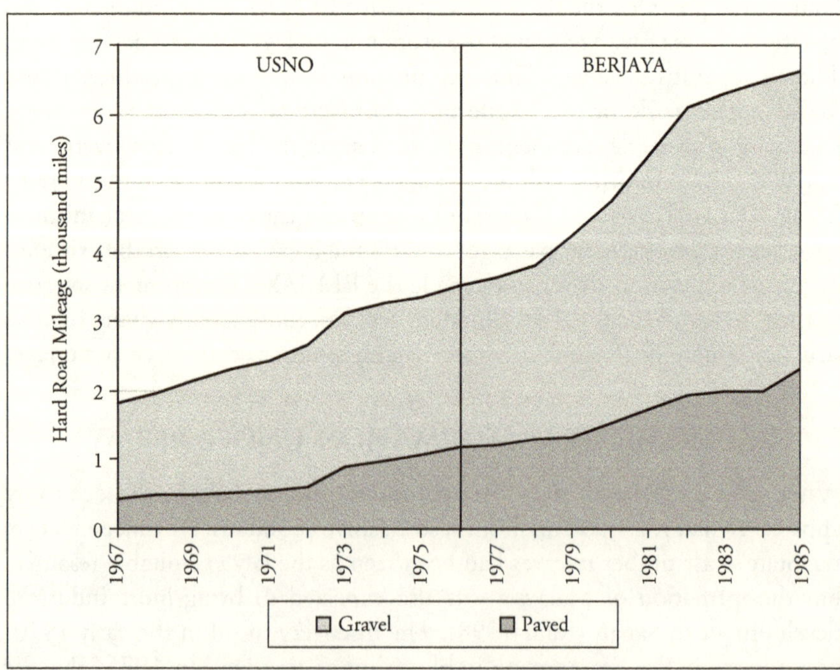

Source: Buku Tahunan Perangkaan Sabah (various years).

Table 5.1
Sectoral Contribution to GDP in Sabah and Malaysia, 1970–85

	1970	1975	1980	1985
Primary Sector	52.9 (37.8)	48.4 (33.8)	55.3 (32.8)	54.7 (30.4)
Secondary Sector	8.7 (16.7)	9.9 (19.0)	8.3 (24.6)	9.6 (24.3)
Tertiary Sector	38.4 (45.5)	41.7 (47.2)	36.4 (42.6)	35.7 (45.3)

Note: Figures for Malaysia in brackets.
Source: Buku Tahunan Perangkaan Sabah (various years).

shortest possible time can have few parallels anywhere".[4] On face value, the party did indeed appear to have a lot to boast about. By 1980, BERJAYA had successfully increased the State's funds from 6 million ringgit, at the end of 1975, to nearly 12 billion.[5] Poverty was down by almost half, to 33.1 per cent in 1984. Infrastructural development had also proceeded apace. Between 1967 and 1975, the USNO Administrations had built an average of 189 miles of paved or gravelled roads per year; between 1976 and 1984, BERJAYA built on average 346 miles per year (see Figure 5.1).

Yet Sabah's economy had still not significantly diversified. With the increasing role of oil in the economy, the primary sector's contribution to the State's GDP had increased, while the secondary sector had at best stagnated, remaining below the 10 per cent mark. In comparison, by 1985, the secondary sector accounted for roughly a quarter of Malaysia's overall GDP (see Table 5.1). Unemployment in Sabah had also spiralled under BERJAYA. In 1975, unemployment in Sabah was 4.7 per cent, compared to 7.4 per cent on the Peninsula. By 1985, unemployment in Sabah had more or less doubled to 9.3 per cent, above the Peninsula's rate of 8.1 per cent.

THE POLITICAL ECONOMY OF BERJAYA: TIMBER AND THE ABC SYSTEM

In understanding the political economic strategy of BERJAYA, a key issue — both for the Sabah economy and as an arena in which this strategy was at its clearest — was the timber industry. The BERJAYA policy towards timber was indicative of the broader political economy, in that it mixed policy measures, seeking to utilize resources for wide-ranging development, with an increasing patronage structure that underlined its development agenda.

Timber played a significant role in the political economy of Sabah and, therefore, had always been a contentious issue in Sabah politics. As a main source of income, it contributed 50 per cent of the State's gross national product, formed 57 per cent of exports and employed 25 per cent of the workforce in 1975.[6] With the earliest record of logging activities stretching back to 1885, a considerable area in the west coast forest had been logged to the point of exhaustion. When Sabah was under the Colonial Government, the British created a system of granting timber concessions to key leaders representing their respective ethnic communities. Mustapha, Fuad Stephens, G.S. Sundang and Khoo Siak Chew were each granted timber concessions for forty square miles to fund their political activities (Granville-Edge 2002, p. 92).

Under the USNO regime, the issuance of new timber licences was the domain of a handful of elite politicians and wealthy Chinese businessmen. When BERJAYA took over the government, these financial privileges became instrumental to the institutional expansion and the creation of ambitious leaders in the BERJAYA Government. One of the major policy changes in timber made by Harris Salleh, as the new Chief Minister of Sabah, was to reduce log export by 50 per cent in stages, between 1976 and 1982, to stem the destruction of Sabah's forests — a resource that takes up to eighty years to replace.[7] This was followed by the creation of the Sabah Forest Development Authority (SAFODA), which carried out reforestation and resettlement programmes in Sabah and the withdrawal of several timber concessions. Harris cancelled the timber licences issued by Mustapha, amounting to 810,319 acres of forestland. No compensation was paid to the concession holders and Harris stressed that, "A license is not a property under Article 13 of the Malaysian Constitution — it is only a privilege and this can be cancelled at any time."[8]

Harris denied the allegation that the cancellation of timber licences was a way of transferring forestry privileges from the USNO party to his own. Indeed, to some extent, the BERJAYA timber policies did appear to be aimed at conserving this valuable resource for the benefit of all Sabahans. About half of the acreage cancelled was given to the Rural Development Corporation (KPD), a government-sponsored agency that granted credit to farmers to improve their agricultural techniques, and the remaining acreage to the Sabah Foundation. Harris claimed that no more timber concessions were issued after 1978. The government had instead bought over timber concessions held by smallholders in the interior and reorganized them into large plots of up to 300,000 acres, to be developed jointly by both local and foreign companies.[9] The consolidated approach to the development of cash crop plantation involved the clearing and extraction of interior forests, ultimately creating permanent settlements for former shifting cultivators through SAFODA, under the management of the Sabah Land Development Board (SLDB).

Despite these positive measures in forestry management, the BERJAYA Government apparently could not resist the allocation of timber licences to well-connected individuals. Of the USNO-awarded licences cancelled in 1977, a proportion not developed under State-sponsored schemes (around one half) was allocated to 1,500 individuals, of whom 1,300 were *bumiputeras* and the remainder Chinese; this was in sharp contrast to the previous situation in which the majority of the timber concession holders in Sabah were wealthy Chinese.[10] The 1,500 recipients of timber licences, covering 43,000 acres of cancelled concessions, were selected "according to their standing in their district, politically, as community leaders and as business-minded people"; this was also one of the main rewards of becoming leaders in the BERJAYA party, according to the so-called "ABC system".[11] The ABC system was a way of grading community leaders — who were also BERJAYA party members — according to their social status in society. The distribution of timber licences through the ABC system became the means by which community leaders could fulfil their 'political obligations' to their respective communities.[12]

Applying for large tracts of land for agricultural development usually became the standard practice of BERJAYA members within the ABC system. In one land application letter produced by the Chief Minister's Department, dated 26 January 1979, addressed to specific party members at the Kundasang BERJAYA office, the application for 5,000 acres of land in Sandakan — fifty acres per person — for the purposes of agricultural development was approved.[13] The approval was given under Part II of the Country Lands Ordinance Chapter 68 with regard to land clearance for agricultural purposes, which also stated that, if such areas contained timber, the usual extraction fee and royalty charges would be applicable. Applicants were also advised to refer to the Forestry Department in relation to the issuance of timber licences.[14] The applicants were members of the *Wanita* BERJAYA, who were based in Kundasang. Land application was one of the political obligations that the BERJAYA leaders performed for their respective communities and it was through the ABC system that institutional patronage began to take shape under the BERJAYA party.

THE INSTITUTIONAL EXPANSION OF BERJAYA CORPORATE GOVERNANCE

Beyond the realm of timber, the political economy of the BERJAYA Government was elsewhere also a mix of development and patronage. The institutional expansion of BERJAYA was aided by the Sabah Foundation and the establishment of cooperatives as a strategy of development. The reduction in log exports did not have a huge impact upon the structural distribution of timber concessions, nor on the problems associated with timber politics. The ABC system of the BERJAYA party did not differ from the practices of the previous government. Under USNO, political patronage was linked to the establishment of the Sabah Foundation. As Chief Minister, Mustapha had control over all civil service appointments and timber concessions. The Ministry of Natural Resources was abolished in 1967 and was put under the Chief Minister's Department, together with the government tenders board.[15] The Sabah Foundation was formed in 1967 with a 1 million ringgit grant awarded by the State Government, and 3,300 square miles of forest to finance its operations. Mustapha, who was the Chief Minister, was the Chairman of the Sabah Foundation, whilst Syed Kechik was the first Managing Director (Raffaele 1986, p. 172). The Sabah Foundation was a non-profit organization designed to promote social and educational developments in Sabah, and timber was its main source of funding for this purpose. In 1970, a total of 8,547 square kilometres of timber concession land had been granted to the Sabah Foundation, and companies established and owned by the Sabah Foundation were given the right to exploit timber forests awarded by the Sabah Government (Ross-Larson 1974). Under Mustapha, the Sabah Foundation became a strategic instrument for State exploitation and administration of timber resources, with timber concessions distributed as political pay-offs to his supporters (Means 1991, p. 42).

In the attempt to dismantle the legacy of Mustapha, Harris Salleh put the non-profit organization directly under the jurisdiction of the government, with the aim of making it more accountable.[16] Under Harris, the image of the Sabah Foundation was reinvented to become that of a corporate giant, undertaking joint ventures in timber exploitation, commercial forestry plantation and sawmill operation, with both local and foreign companies. The Sabah Foundation's timber areas were consolidated in 1984, bringing its total area to 9,728 square kilometres, and the Sabah Foundation Forest Management Plan (1984–2032), a scheme approved by the Sabah Government, began to undertake the management of the consolidated forestland. In 1977, the Sabah Foundation generated about 125 million ringgit in revenue from timber.

The Sabah State Government received about 35 per cent in taxes and royalty payments. The extraction charges to logging contractors amounted to 34 per cent, a further 14 per cent was tied to the joint ventures, and 10 per cent was charged to the Sabah Foundation's administration. Despite the Sabah Foundation's emphasis on social development, social programmes actually accounted for less than 10 per cent of the timber revenue spent in 1977.[17]

Logging activities, SAFODA reforestation and resettlement projects did not yield the intended results. Estimates of the area annually cut in Sabah fell from 3,640 square kilometres in 1978 to more than 2,000 square kilometres a decade later — a loss of 30 per cent of forestland from 1970 to 1989.[18] Chandler's (1989) study of the Nabawan resettlement scheme revealed that whilst the Sabah Government had taken a consultative approach towards shifting cultivation in its rural development plan, the lack of infrastructural support underlined the 'bias' affecting access to agricultural development projects among the rural population in general. The SAFODA settlement scheme failed to keep pace with the reforestation effort and, by 1987, the 34 SLDB schemes housed only 2,748 settler families on 52,289 hectares, fewer than were housed on a smaller area of land in 1980 (Brookfield et al. 1995). Apparently, the native people of Sabah were reluctant to accept the kind of land settlement discipline founded on the West Malaysian model (Sutton 1989). Reports of settlers' dissatisfaction were quite common and, in one instance, the settlers in the Sungai Manila Scheme tied up their manager when they were not given their salaries.[19] The land schemes proved to be unpopular among Sabahans and, by the 1980s, three groups of settlement schemes were almost without settler families. These settlements failed to work in a large-scale capacity and were sustained only on a plantation-estate basis, using immigrants from the Philippines and Indonesia as the principal source of labour. By 1986, foreign workers from these two countries formed ninety per cent of the labour force in the Sabah agriculture and plantation economy, and almost half the workforce in forestry (Pang 1990).

The Sabah Foundation's pledge to share its wealth with Sabahans was employed through the distribution of cash dividends, called the *Amanah Saham Tun Hj. Datu Mustapha* (later renamed *Amanah Rakyat Sabah*), to the entire native-born population in Sabah, above the age of twenty-one — in essence, the voting public.[20] The idea was to ensure a more equitable distribution of Sabah's timber wealth among the Sabah population. Under USNO, 50 ringgit was granted to 182,000 beneficiaries in 1971. The amount was increased to 60 ringgit in 1973 for 249,000 and again in 1974 for 258,000 beneficiaries. When the Parliamentary election in 1978 was due in July, the BERJAYA Government did not hesitate to announce a 'windfall' of

80 ringgit for the 315,000 beneficiaries of the *Amanah Saham Rakyat,* five months ahead of the polls.[21] By the following year, Harris was urging the 'rich and well-to-do' to give up their *Amanah Rakyat Sabah* dividends in favour of school grants for the needy.[22] The last distribution of the cash dividend was in 1981, a few months ahead of the Sabah State election, and the amount given was 150 ringgit to more than a quarter of a million beneficiaries above the age of twenty-one. By 1981, the Sabah Foundation had spent a total sum of 10.5 million ringgit on *Amanah Rakyat Sabah* and the Foundation was forced to cut down its spending on social programmes due to dwindling market prices and the high cost of production in the timber industry.[23]

Economic growth in Sabah depended mainly on timber, and the Sabah Foundation apparently had a 'mind of its own' when it came to funding projects and programmes outside of the government.[24] Under BERJAYA, the Sabah Foundation's commitment to social and educational development was nebulous but there were notable changes to its policies, particularly in utilizing forest revenues for various projects related to the BERJAYA party. The BERJAYA Government expanded the economic functions of the Sabah Foundation in such a way that it changed the role of the Sabah Foundation from that of a non-profit organization to a semi-government corporate institution. Rightly or wrongly, the Sabah Foundation generated the conditions for timber politics and patronage, and the Mustapha legacy continued to flourish under the BERJAYA Government.

POCKETS OF PATRONAGE: THE ROLES OF THE COOPERATIVES

UMNO's cooperative movement, *Koperasi Usaha Bersatu Malaysia Sdn Bhd* (BERSATU), inspired BERJAYA to establish its own cooperative movement in 1976, called the *Koperasi BERJAYA Bhd* (KOBERSA). KOBERSA was the investment arm of the BERJAYA party and had considerable equity in Stephens Properties Sdn Bhd, had acquired eighteen per cent shares in Kinabalu Motor Assembly, and was planning to develop 110 acres of housing in Putatan, which was to be named the 'Taman BERJAYA'.[25] In 1979, KOBERSA and BERSATU established a joint company called the *Syarikat Jaya Usaha Bersatu Sdn Bhd* (JUB), with the sole aim of bringing the two political parties into an economic alliance.[26] The joint venture was incorporated in Kuala Lumpur with an authorized capital of 10 million ringgit and chaired by the Secretary-General of BN, Ghafar Baba (Gale 1986, p. 36). The establishment of KOBERSA provided the impetus for the formation of various cooperative societies under BERJAYA. These cooperatives provided employment and economic opportunities for BERJAYA's existing members and were an incentive for people to join and support BERJAYA.

In line with the goal of the NEP, the BERJAYA Government expanded the role of the Sabah Economic Development Corporation (SEDCO) to increase *bumiputera* capital ownership and economic participation. SEDCO was established in 1971 by the USNO Government as the investment arm of the Sabah Government in facilitating industrial and manufacturing development in Sabah. By 1983, it had invested about 324.6 million ringgit in various development programmes. In 1977, the *Bumiputera* Participation Unit was established with the aim of increasing *bumiputera* involvement in trade and industry. Along with this, in 1980, the BERJAYA Government gave 150 million ringgit to *Permodalan Bumiputera Sabah* to invest in finance, hotels and property development on behalf of the *bumiputera* community (Gudgeon 1981, p. 334). The integrated functions of the Sabah Foundation, SEDCO and the *Bumiputera* Chamber of Commerce facilitated the economic expansion of these government-funded agencies underlining the strategy for rural development in Sabah. These cooperatives played the role of organizing smallholders in the rural areas and creating production and marketing agencies for their products.

The BERJAYA Government reorganized these cooperative societies for their political benefit. BERJAYA took over the administration of the Sabah National Youth Association (SANYA), an organization that had served to strengthen Mustapha's position in the 1960s. Mustapha and a key civil servant, Dzulkifli Hamid, headed the organization that claimed to have 60,000 members by the 1970s. SANYA played a key role in undermining the network of the Kadazan Youth, a cultural organization established during Donald Stephens' time, and was also responsible for the break-up of the Sabah Association of Chinese Youth Clubs.[27] The reorganization of SANYA was politically significant for BERJAYA because it was a potential source of political support in return for employment opportunities for SANYA members.

Under BERJAYA, the SANYA Multi-Purpose Cooperative Bhd (KOSAN) was set up in 1976 to provide training programmes and employment opportunities for its members. Funded by the government, KOSAN became involved in textiles, shoes, plastics, manufacturing, printing, distributing gems and property development (Gudgeon 1981, p. 334). KOSAN made school uniforms and shoes, which the BERJAYA Government provided free of charge to all primary and secondary schools via the Sabah Foundation. When Harris issued a decree in December 1983 requiring all civil servants to wear uniforms, KOSAN was the outlet for civil servants to purchase their materials for the uniform.[28] KOSAN had a marketing subsidiary, called the KOSAN Marketing Agency (KOSMA), set up in 1982 as a body to ensure the marketability of KOSAN-made products for domestic and international markets. However, KOSMA was relatively short-lived and was closed down after two years.[29]

In the wholesale and retail trade, *Koperasi Jelata Sabah* (KOJASA) was set up in 1978 to operate low-price supermarket shops (Gudgeon 1981, p. 335). After four years in business, however, the KOJASA retail outlets did not do as well as anticipated. As a way of encouraging people to patronize the KOJASA outlets in Kota Kinabalu, Harris ordered the Municipal Council to divert traffic flow away from other shops, to make way for an extra seventy parking lots for KOJASA shoppers.[30] This move prompted objections from the business community and the Kota Kinabalu Municipal Council on the grounds that these directives were impractical.[31] In the end, the plan never materialized.

Koperasi Pembangunan Desa (KPD) was set up in 1976 to improve the agricultural production and livestock development of rural communities. Similarly, Sabah Marketing Agencies (SAMA) was set up to market this produce. The *Koperasi Serbaguna Nelayan Sabah Bhd* (KO-NELAYAN) was established in 1978 with 50 million ringgit in grants to provide loans to fishermen and to improve the working conditions of the fishing community. KPD and KO-NELAYAN achieved moderate success compared to other agencies and were brought under the supervision of the Ministry of Agriculture and Fishery in the early 1980s. All these agencies, except for KPD and KO-NELAYAN, were coordinated by *Koperasi Rakyat Sabah Bhd* (KORAS), another government-funded agency that provided management training for officers of cooperative societies on how to run their respective organizations.

Almost all these agencies were financially supported by the Sabah Government and politically linked to BERJAYA. These cooperatives were aimed at improving the economic conditions of people in Sabah by creating greater business and employment opportunities for the *bumiputera* in rural Sabah. However, they had become politically entangled with BERJAYA, fuelling the patronage network within the party by giving material benefits to those supporting or linked to the BERJAYA Government. The biggest industrial investor in Sabah, SEDCO, did not do very well at the time despite spending about 80 million ringgit in the manufacturing sector. SEDCO had seventeen operating subsidiaries and associates in the manufacturing sector, which included motor assembly, paint processing, shipbuilding, flour and feed milling, brick-making, and cement production. Of the seventeen enterprises, only the cement works, one brick factory and one trading company had a profitable record.[32] The vehicle plant, Kinabalu Motor Assembly, was set up in 1979 to assemble Isuzu trucks. However, the plant was only working at 25 per cent capacity, selling 1,268 cars, which comprised only 23 per cent of the market in the previous year. By 1982, the company was making a loss of 3 million ringgit.[33] Shocked by these figures, Harris immediately directed all government departments and government-funded agencies to purchase only Isuzu trucks assembled locally, and for government-owned finance companies to finance Isuzu trucks exclusively.[34] Later that year, the Internal Auditor's investigation into *Perusahaan Kinabalu Motor* (Perkina) revealed massive irregularities and fraud amounting to losses of 8 million ringgit.[35] All in all, it had incurred a total loss of 16 million ringgit since it started.[36]

The *Bumiputera* Participation Unit (BPU), later renamed the *Pribumi* Participation Unit, was set up in 1977 to encourage the participation of native communities in commerce and industry (*Bumiputera* Participation Unit [n.d.]). It accumulated debts amounting to 80 million ringgit after six years in operation.[37] Harris appointed a ten-member committee to deliberate on the issue but announced that the committee "be asked to make a political decision on whether the outstanding debts could be written off instead of a decision by the State government".[38] There were a total of seventy persons involved in this debt and Harris said that, "if the Government went ahead and took action against the individuals concerned, it could be accused of not being considerate".[39] Later, Harris made a different statement on the *pribumi* debtors, saying that the Sabah government would take "*pribumi* debtors who are owing the State government to court", when a report on 1 October 1983 issued by the Chief Minister's Department exposed a total of 1,598 *pribumi* owing a sum of 104.4 million ringgit to the government.[40] This shifting position with regard to the *pribumi* debts gave rise to the idea that some debtors were more deserving of being let off than others.

The lack of assertiveness on the part of the BERJAYA leadership in monitoring the accountability and transparency in institutional governance resulted in a string of high profile corruption cases involving government officers and government-funded agencies in the 1980s. Several officers, including the acting Director of the Welfare Department, were involved in a 4 million ringgit scandal in connection with relief aid earmarked for flood victims in the period 1980–81.[41] The main charges included the approval of ten payments for amounts ranging from 60,000 ringgit to 80,000 ringgit to companies that falsely claimed they had provided food and relief supplies to flood victims. Labuk Assemblyman Paul Baklin bin Gurandi was also charged with graft for making a false claim of 43,000 ringgit as payment for KORAS. An ex-District Officer of Tuaran, Awang Yahya Ahmad Shah, was arrested for making a false claim of 2,320 ringgit as payment for the *Majlis Ugama Islam Sabah* (MUIS).[42] Another individual, the financial officer of MUIS, Idris Harun, received a five-year jail sentence and 10,000 ringgit fine by the Sessions Court for criminal breach of trust involving 503,241 ringgit.[43]

Some of the cooperatives set up by BERJAYA were also implicated in graft and other corrupt acts. The Sabah Marketing Cooperative (SAMA) accumulated a loss of 19 million ringgit in 1982 and its executive was arrested for corruption totalling 75,000 ringgit in 1984; the manager of KORAS was charged for making a false claim totalling 66,376 ringgit in 1984; in the same year, three other officers were arrested for corruption totalling 56,650 ringgit in a scandal involving SAFODA and the Sabah Credit Corporation; the top executive officers of KOJASA, SAMA and MUIS were arrested on graft charges.[44] These government agencies were an important part of the rural development programme of the BERJAYA Government, but their roles in modernizing rural life became questionable in the light of these corruption cases.

THE PLEDGE FOR POLITICAL LOYALTY: THE JKK

In 1975, the *Jawatankuasa Kemajuan Kampung* (JKK, or Village Development Committee, later renamed the *Jawatankuasa Keselamatan dan Kemajuan Kampung*, JKKK) was established as part of the rural development programme under the NEP to redress rural poverty in Sabah (Jabatan Ketua Menteri 1975). The JKK members came from the village community and were presided over by the village headman or the Native Chief. "In order to provide our people more guidance and support, the ruling Party is among other things strengthening the system of Pemimpin Kemajuan Rakyat to involve more BERJAYA leaders in our development efforts at the grass-roots level" (Harris Mohd. Salleh 1981, p. 20). The *Pemimpin Kemajuan Rakyat* (PKR, or Community Development Officer, CDO) was a government-appointed position that supervised the administrative machinery of the JKK. The PKR was therefore responsible for submitting any proposal or application for village development that had been approved by the JKK.

The roles of the Native Chiefs and the village headmen as community leaders had evolved over time, and, in the context of Sabah politics, these Native Chiefs and village headmen were known to have significant links to the government and the people at the grass-roots level. Under USNO, they had to sign a pledge of loyalty to the government. With USNO's ouster, these community leaders were made to pledge their loyalty to the BERJAYA party instead. In fact, many of the leaders were persuaded to pledge their loyalty to BERJAYA even before BERJAYA came to power.[45] Apparently, this pledge of loyalty had been obtained under threat of denial of development funds should BERJAYA come to power.

The BERJAYA Government set up short training courses and seminars for these community leaders in order to update them on government policies, as well as to guide them on how to manage village affairs.[46] The District Officers and Native Chiefs were also sent to Peninsular Malaysia and Sarawak for training purposes.[47] Indeed, the burden of village progress and development rested squarely on their shoulders. As the State Minister of Finance, Mohd Noor Mansoor, declared when he addressed the Native Chiefs and village headmen in 1977, "Whether a village develops or not, it depends heavily on your initiative."[48]

Under the BERJAYA Government, the JKK projected an image of itself as a community-based organization but actually it functioned as a political unit at the village level. The reorganization of the JKKs was carried out under the Chief Minister's Department in September 1982; this gave the JKK more authority in monitoring and recommending development projects and functioning as the government at the village level.[49] The BERJAYA Government further insisted that it would not entertain official requests of any kind from the people (except for those regarding employment) unless recommended by the JKK. The new ruling applied to applications for land, permits to construct houses, trading and firearms licences, replanting grants, loans from public financial institutions, education scholarships, and other applications requiring the approval of government departments or agencies.[50] The ruling also imposed certain conditions on the setting-up of a JKK, whereby only villages with village headmen were eligible to form the JKK and villages without headmen would need to consult with the nearest village that had a JKK.

The reorganization of the JKK in 1982 had excluded certain villages that did not have village headmen or which were in opposition strongholds. The then Assistant Minister of Resource Development, Yapin Gimpoton, stressed that the "BERJAYA government and its leaders should leave Usukan and its people alone", when the BERJAYA candidate was defeated by USNO in the Usukan by-election.[51] When Sandakan Municipal Councillors appealed for clean water to be supplied to drought victims in rural areas, they were told to personally bear the costs of transportation. Indeed, Sandakan's development was arrested when it voted again for the opposition DAP in the 1981 general election. When villages in Sandakan experienced problems with their water supply, the BERJAYA Government seemed to take the attitude that Sandakan's problems were the opposition's problems.

Apart from being a conduit between the local community and the development agency, the role of the JKK was considerable as a strategy of political control. How and to what extent the JKK was harnessed for this purpose is well exemplified in the following court case. The case was reported in the *Daily Express*. On 17 February 1982, the High Court began the hearing of the first of the twenty election petitions filed by an USNO election agent, seeking to nullify the election of the BERJAYA Assemblyman for Kawang, Fred Sinidol, on grounds of alleged corrupt practices and undue influence during the Sabah State election in March 1981. The main issue in the petition centred on how, out of 717,000 ringgit distributed under the Kampung Rehabilitation Scheme in Kawang in March 1981, only 61,000 ringgit were accounted for in receipts; the payment scheme therefore did not comply with the Treasury's instructions.[52] The funds for the Kampung Rehabilitation Scheme in Kawang were meant for poor villagers to repair their houses and for the construction of public utilities. The court was also told that just before the election, a warrant authorizing 816,000 ringgit from the Chief Minister's Department for the scheme in Kawang was approved. All applications under the scheme were made to the JKK with the endorsement of the CDO.[53]

One of the witnesses was Mallin Manjitar, the CDO and BERJAYA Divisional Secretary for the Kawang constituency. He admitted to receiving 60,000 ringgit on behalf of several groups of people applying for assistance under the scheme before the 1981 State election.[54] Mallin admitted that payments of 10,000 ringgit each were given to the village headmen who normally chaired the JKK in their respective villages, and who happened to be BERJAYA members. When the leading counsel for the petition, Dominic Puthucheary, questioned the criteria for providing assistance, Mallin simply said that the economic status of the applicant was not an issue as civil servants and police also qualified for assistance and all he did was to endorse the applications submitted by the JKK. Puthucheary produced a 'vote book' detailing a record of applicants who received aid and highlighted many names who were apparently close relatives of Mallin. In the list of successful applicants, Mohd Zain Kinsung, a Native Chief, received three aid packages totalling 14,300 ringgit on a single day in March 1981, and an officer in the Treasury Department, Antin Joseph, received 7,500 ringgit. Mallin could not give reasons as to why these huge amounts were given to individuals and denied the charge that he was instructed to cancel applications from USNO members.[55]

A former CDO and also BERJAYA party Divisional Secretary of Kawang, Asek bin Pintar, told the court that he was removed from his position because he did not follow Fred Sinidol's instructions to stop giving development aid or other forms of government assistance to USNO supporters.[56] A farmer, Teddy Sindu, testified that when Fred Sinidol was the Chairman of the Sabah Electricity Board (SEB) in 1980, the power supply to the households of opposition supporters was cut off. When he inquired about this inconsistency in the power supply at the SEB office in Papar, he was told that he could not get electricity supplied because of a strong objection filed by the JKK. The power supply to Teddy Sindu's house was finally restored only after he wrote to Deputy Prime Minister Musa Hitam, the Sabah Chief Minister and the Minster of Infrastructure Development.[57]

The hearings also produced witnesses aged between 64 and 89 years who testified that their monthly allowance of 60 ringgit under the Old Age Assistance Scheme was stopped after May 1981 upon the discovery that they were USNO supporters.[58] When the State Minister of Community Service, Rahimah Stephens, finally appeared in court after several subpoenas, she defended the directive to cancel the Old Age Assistance Scheme funding for 138 elderly on the basis that they each possessed properties worth more than 1,000 ringgit. Her explanation contradicted an earlier testimony by the Permanent Secretary and Welfare Services Director who had said that they were not given any reason for the cancellation of the aid, contrary to Rahimah's claim.[59]

When it came to the issue of funding approval, the Director of Audit, Philip Wong, testified that the fast application and the approval of 816,000 ringgit on the same day was not something unusual, and it could be done on the same day in the case of an emergency. The application for 816,000 ringgit was submitted on 17 February 1981 and the approval was given on the following day, 18 February 1981; this allocation was made out to the District Office but for the use of the Kawang constituency.[60] Wong further testified that he was not aware of any internal audit carried out on the 816,000 ringgit spent on the Kawang constituency.[61] State Development Officer Mahfar Sairan testified that Sabah was the only state in the country which provided its own funds under the Village Rehabilitation Scheme but, as far as building houses and upgrading the village were concerned, he stated that the materials could only be purchased by the District Officer or a government-appointed contractor; he further emphasized that the money could not be paid out to any individual to purchase materials or to conduct repairs himself.[62]

Puthucheary rested his case after a forty-six day hearing, during which time a total of sixty-four witnesses testified in court. The leading counsel for Fred Sinidol, Raja Aziz Addruse, sought an adjournment until the next day when he submitted that his client had no case to answer. The reason given was that the petition was akin to a criminal case, which inevitably prevented Fred Sinidol from standing in the witness box. This notice caught Puthucheary by surprise, who then retorted that the counsel was trying to put them in the position of a prosecutor, whilst denying them the facilities of a prosecution.[63] Justice Chong Siew Fai permitted the 'no case to answer' application by the BERJAYA counsel on the grounds that, in both criminal and civil cases, the course of submitting a 'no case to answer' application was open to the defendant.[64] In submitting the USNO versus BERJAYA election petition, Raja Aziz insisted that the court must consider the standard of proof equivalent to that in a criminal trial and stressed that the people should not file election petitions on frivolous and scandalous grounds. He then urged the court to dismiss the petition arguing that the petitioner had failed to prove the charges against the respondent "beyond reasonable doubt".[65]

After forty-nine days of deliberation, the trial judge, Chong Siew Fai, dismissed the election petition and declared that the petitioner had failed to establish any of the charges of bribery and undue influence, stating that "[n]o case had been established to the satisfaction of the court justifying the declaration that the election in the Kawang constituency at the March 1981 State assembly election of Sabah is void".[66] On the evidence that the Old Age Assistance funds of a number of persons appeared to have been unjustifiably terminated in May 1981, he ruled that the terminations were irrelevant to the charges in the petition, and that the termination happened after the election, hence it was not proven to have any connection with the exercise of any electoral right or voting in the election.

The election petition hearing had revealed the extent to which the JKK had been politicized and even used for political surveillance at the village level. Evidently the JKK had assumed the role of recommending to the BERJAYA leaders who in the village ought to, or ought not to, be given aid and this on the basis of whether one was a BERJAYA or opposition party supporter. As in the case related to the termination of the Old Age Assistance funds, the Welfare Minister, Rahimah Stephens, had to be reminded by Puthucheary that there was no need for her to accept the advice of the JKK (an organization that had no statutory existence); "Our system of government is that ministers must act in accordance with the law".[67]

In its attempt to reorganize its power base and to reward its supporters, the BERJAYA Government used the JKK to penetrate to the local level. Consequently, the JKK's role as a conduit linking rural development projects undertaken by the government to the local villagers was transformed into that of a political machine rewarding only BERJAYA supporters, while restricting development projects in opposition strongholds. It is undeniable that Sabah experienced relatively rapid development under the BERJAYA Government, but the network of patronage became more widespread and extended downwards to include village headmen and Native Chiefs too.

With the introduction of a modern political system, particularly that of the JKK, Lasimbang (2002) argued that the significance of the traditional institution of authority was gradually being undermined. In charting the patterns of traditional leadership in Malaya, Syed Husin Ali (1968) suggested that once the *penghulu* (headmen) were drafted into the State apparatus, their traditional leadership role changed from being *orang kita* (one of us) to being *orang Kerajaan* (the government's men), assuming their role at the bottom rung in the State Administration, as brokers between the villagers at the grass-roots level and State officials (Chee 1974). For some village headmen, the politics of patronage had transformed their role from that of the traditional bearer of justice for the village community to that of a part-time politician bearing instructions from the government on the business of administering the village community. The Chairmen of the JKK, who happened to be village headmen or Native Chiefs, became the points of access and instruments for rewarding or punishing those villagers who either supported or opposed the BERJAYA Government correspondingly. The pledge of loyalty to BERJAYA was used to tie Native Chiefs and village headmen to BERJAYA's political patronage, thus entrenching politically-oriented development policies in rural development.

CONCLUSION

Harris was convinced that BERJAYA's second electoral victory was attributable to the people's acceptance of "our development-oriented policies, our style of Government and our [multiracial] concept" (Harris Mohd. Salleh 1981, p. 15). However, BERJAYA had inherited a considerable part of USNO's legacy of political patronage that had been built upon the Sabah Foundation. Instead of dismantling the Mustapha legacy, the BERJAYA Government extended and actually entrenched political patronage to a wider circle of community leaders, in particular Native Chiefs and village headmen.

It cannot be denied that, under Harris, Sabah's economy bounced back on the course of development. However, the bulk of revenue from the Sabah economy, and consequently the funding for the formation of early political parties, came solely from timber. The economic and also political reliance on timber eventually became contentious, particularly with regard to how these timber licences were issued. Under the BERJAYA Government, the ABC system was employed in allocating timber licences to politicians, community leaders and favoured businessmen. Harris defended this system because he believed that this system would empower individual leaders to fulfil their political obligations in their respective communities. Harris' Government also attempted several positive measures to achieve sustainable forest management but these efforts were overshadowed by the network of patronage and personal interests involved in the issuance of forest licences.

Under BERJAYA, the Sabah Foundation was responsible for the overall management of the forests, although the specific tasks of reforestation and the management of settlement schemes were delegated to SAFODA and SLDB respectively. Apart from distributing *Amanah Saham Rakyat Sabah* dividends to Sabahans, BERJAYA also linked the activities of the Sabah Foundation to various government cooperative agencies, supplementing the development strategies of the BERJAYA Government. Harris explained that mismanagement and incompetence were the main causes for the underperformance of these cooperative agencies.[68] In reality, graft, corruption and patronage set in too, and indirectly contributed to their failure.

The ABC system of the BERJAYA Government was an example of how government and party roles overlapped in the course of carrying out development projects. In effect, it created selected development for certain groups of people loyal to the BERJAYA Government. Such selective development was extended down to the JKK — the government at the village level. The policy of selective development became apparent after BERJAYA suffered a humiliating defeat in the Sandakan constituency in the 1978 and 1982 general elections. In an attempt to maintain and regain political support, selective development programmes were employed to reward supporters and punish those who opposed the government. In this context, the JKK provided the best avenue for the BERJAYA Government to reward only its hard core supporters, with the hope that those in the opposition camps would return to BERJAYA out of desperation.

The politics of development had inadvertently transformed the role of village headmen. The role of Native Chiefs and the village headmen as bearers of justice at the village level, especially during British times, was gradually transformed by the politics of patronage and the modern day requirements of a part-time politician. On the one hand, the politics of development had achieved a modicum of acceptance and, to a certain extent, legitimacy, among certain groups of people. On the other hand, these tactics led to feelings of discontent and disenchantment among others, as the petition hearing showed. However, this alone may only provide a partial understanding of BERJAYA politics because there was still the issue of cultural and religious identity with which the BERJAYA Government had to deal.

Notes

1. *Daily Express*, 7 March 1979.
2. Ibid., 7 April 1982.
3. Ibid., 3 March 1982.
4. *Far Eastern Economic Review*, 14 April 1983.
5. *Daily Express*, 1 October 1981.
6. *Far Eastern Economic Review*, 14 January 1977.
7. Ibid., 2 December 1977.
8. Ibid., 2 December 1977
9. Ibid., 30 November 1979.
10. Ibid., 2 December 1977.
11. The ABC system was a way of rewarding the leaders and some 'outstanding members' within the BERJAYA party. The classification was as follows: 'A' usually for politicians and BERJAYA leaders; 'B' for businessmen; and 'C' for community leaders, Native Chiefs and village headmen. These details were revealed in an interview with Harris Salleh by the author.
12. Harris Salleh, interview by the author, 2003.
13. Chief Minister's Department, 26 January 1979.
14. Chief Minister's Department, 26 January 1979.
15. *Far Eastern Economic Review*, 2 April 1970.
16. Harris Salleh was the Chairman of the Sabah Foundation, whilst Tan Sri Ben Stephens, Donald Stephens' brother, was the Director.
17. *Far Eastern Economic Review*, 24 July 1980.
18. *Malaysian Business*, 1 August 1988; *New Straits Times*, 20 March 1993.
19. *Daily Express*, 11 March 1983.
20. *Far Eastern Economic Review*, 24 July 1980.
21. *Daily Express*, 21 February 1978.
22. Ibid., 18 July 1979.
23. Ibid., 31 August 1981.
24. *Far Eastern Economic Review*, 24 July 1980.
25. Ongkili's speech, no. 46, Terbitan Negeri Sabah, Jabatan Ketua Menteri, 1981.
26. Ibid.
27. *Far Eastern Economic Review*, 2 April 1970.
28. *Daily Express*, 13 September 1983.
29. Ibid., 7 July 1984.
30. Ibid., 19 May 1982.
31. Ibid., 20 May 1982.
32. *Far Eastern Economic Review*, 14 April 1983.

[33] *Daily Express*, 20 May 1982.

[34] Ibid., 20 May 1982.

[35] Perkina Motor Sdn Bhd was the sole agent for Isuzu trucks assembled by the Kinabalu Motor Assembly, which supplied expensive cars and motor vehicles to government departments and agencies. It was a government-owned company with a paid-up capital of about one million shares at $1 each, raised by the *Permodalan bumiputera* in 1979 (*Daily Express*, 21 December 1982).

[36] *Daily Express*, 21 December 1982.

[37] The *Pribumi* Participation Unit shared the objectives of the NEP in eradicating poverty, eliminating the identification of race with economic functions, and encouraging economic development among the *bumiputera* of Sabah (*Daily Express*, 3 May 1983).

[38] Ibid., 3 May 1983.

[39] Ibid., 12 May 1983.

[40] Ibid., 21 October 1983.

[41] Ibid., 5 May 1983.

[42] Ibid., 14 March 1984.

[43] Ibid., 5 September 1984.

[44] Ibid., 23 May 1984; Ibid., 5 January 1984; Ibid., 16 January 1984; Ibid., 8 February 1984.

[45] Ibid., 3 January 1976.

[46] Ibid., 8 January 1977.

[47] Ibid., 3 August 1978.

[48] Ibid., 5 May 1977.

[49] Ibid., 22 October 1982.

[50] Ibid., 28 May 1982.

[51] Ibid., 5 October 1982.

[52] Ibid., 26 May 1982.

[53] Ibid., 27 May 1982.

[54] Ibid., 30 June 1982.

[55] Ibid., 1 July 1982.

[56] Ibid., 14 July 1982.

[57] Ibid., 9 September 1982.

[58] Ibid., 13 July 1982.

[59] Fred Sinidol was Rahima's brother-in-law and she admitted that the JKK gave her a list of persons whose allowance was to be cancelled. When she was asked why she did not liaise with her officers on the matter, she simply replied, "If I feel I should give, I would give and if I don't, I won't." When she was asked if these cancellations were because these people were "USNO member", Rahimah only replied, "The list only mentioned [that they had] opposed the government" (*Daily Express*, 16 September 1982).

[60] *Daily Express*, 18 September 1982.

[61] Ibid., 20 September 1982.

62 Ibid., 24 September 1982.
63 Ibid., 6 October 1982.
64 Ibid., 20 October 1982.
65 Ibid., 9 December 1982.
66 Ibid., 29 April 1983.
67 Ibid., 16 September 1982.
68 Harris Salleh, interview by the author, April 2003.

6

THE CONTEST FOR ISLAMIC LEADERSHIP AND MULTIRACIAL VOTES

INTRODUCTION

The BERJAYA party relied on the concept of 'multiracialism' to bring down the USNO regime in 1976. However, the idea was problematic for the BERJAYA party both at the Federal level and in Sabah itself. Initially, the concept of 'multiracialism' did not appeal to the other dominant pro-Islamic parties, such as UMNO and PAS, within the BN coalition. The BERJAYA party could not draw support from the majority of the Muslim electorate who were strong supporters of USNO in Sabah. This problematic situation for BERJAYA intensified with the advent of the Mahathir Administration at the Federal level, which increasingly moved towards Islamization.

ELECTORAL POLITICS: WHO GOT THE MUSLIM VOTE?

As Milne and Ratnam (1969) observed in their study of voting patterns in the 1967 State elections, the UPKO-USNO contest was expected to, and did, follow broadly ethno-religious lines, with Muslim *bumiputera* generally voting USNO, non-Muslim *bumiputera* voting UPKO, and the Chinese generally — although less consistently — voting SCA. However, it was less easy to advance a similar analysis for the 1976 State election, for two reasons. Firstly, BERJAYA was a new and untested party and it was thus not immediately clear how voters would take to it. Secondly, its espousal of 'multiracialism' clearly demonstrated, at least, the ambition to win votes from more than one community. It was in this latter respect that the initial BERJAYA line-up was notable for its prominent candidates from all the major ethnic and religious groups, including Kadazan Muslim convert Donald Stephens, Christian Kadazan Peter Mojuntin, Muslim *Bumiputera* Harris Salleh, Salleh Sulong, and Chinese Yap Pak Leong.

Unfortunately, ethnic distribution data such as that used by Milne and Ratnam is not available for the 1976 election. However, we can get an idea of the religious breakdown of the vote by looking at the ethnic distribution of the districts — for which census data is available — and comparing this with the aggregate votes received in the State constituencies within the respective districts. Typically, each district contained between two to four State constituencies. Figure 6.1 shows the relationship between the proportion of the population made up of the predominantly non-Muslim groups — the Kadazan, Murut and Chinese — and the proportion of the total vote for BERJAYA in all twenty-one districts.

Figure 6.1
Ethno-religious Voting Patterns, Sabah, 1976

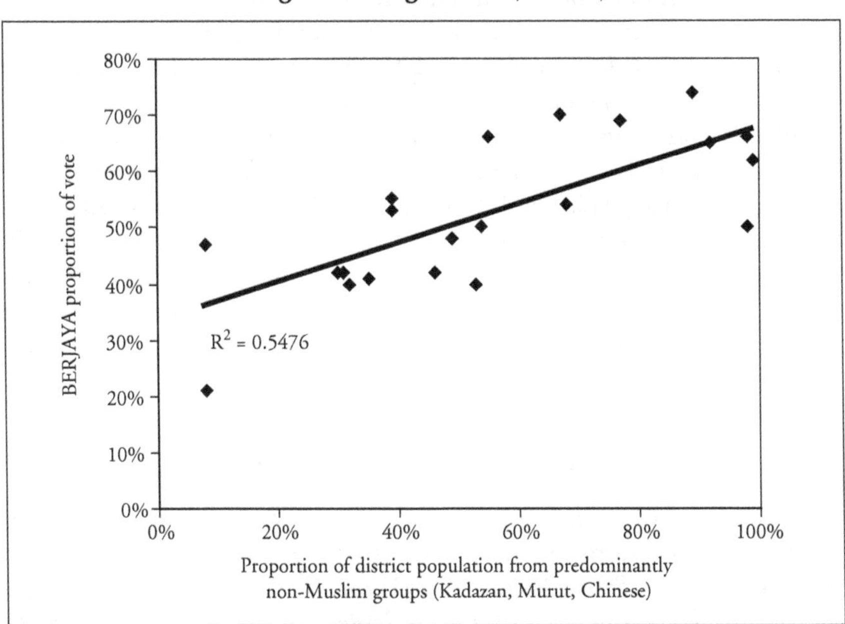

Source: Calculated from 1970 Population and Housing Census (Malaysia 1976) and data provided by Election Commission Sabah.

Figure 6.1 represents the relationship between the proportion of votes for BERJAYA and the percentage of non-Muslim communities in all the districts of Sabah. The graph shows that the percentage of votes for BERJAYA was correspondingly higher in districts that had a higher percentage of non-Muslim voters. The lack of Muslim support for the BERJAYA party meant that their election victory rested on support from the majority non-Muslim communities in Sabah. It could be deduced that the 'multiracial' image of the BERJAYA party attracted votes from non-Muslims which contributed to its 1976 election victory. The non-Muslim communities — particularly the Kadazan-Dusun and Murut — were politically sidelined as a result of UPKO's dissolution in 1967 and the subsequent pro-Islam policies under Mustapha's USNO. The Chinese support for the BERJAYA party was strong, as can be seen when eight SCA candidates lost to BERJAYA in the eight predominantly Chinese constituencies.[1] The concept of 'multiracialism' appealed to the majority non-Muslim electorate mainly because the previous USNO regime promoted pro-Islamic and pro-Malay policies by carrying out mass conversions and abolishing the broadcast of native and Chinese languages over local radio.[2]

BERJAYA's victory in 1976 failed to win substantial support from the Muslim electorate but it did not wish to lose the Islamic leadership to USNO, as this was an important factor with which to close ranks with the dominant party, UMNO, within the BN. The salience of Islamic leadership within the Federal discourse is crucial in understanding how the contest for Islamic leadership between BERJAYA and USNO began to undermine 'multiracialism' in favour of a more Islamized polity. The Islamic resurgence in Peninsular Malaysia in the 1980s considerably contributed to BERJAYA's increasing pro-Islamic outlook and its move to institutionalize Islam in the State Administration. However, BERJAYA's greater identification with Islam undermined its promise to uphold 'multiracialism' in the ethnically complex society of Sabah — a process that contributed to its electoral defeat in 1985.

ISLAMIC MISSIONARY MOVEMENTS

The contest for Islam in Sabah was fought out mainly through competing *Dakwah* organizations allied to various parties and individuals in the State. The United Sabah Islamic Association (USIA) was established as a non-governmental organization on 16 September 1969 with the purpose of developing the Islamic faith within the Sabah population. USIA was established through the amalgamation of Islamic organizations established in the 1940s and 1950s in Sabah (Ismail Yusoff 2004). The Sabah Foundation funded the activities of USIA when Tun Mustapha was still the Chairman of the Foundation. Its efforts, and those of others, had led to some important conversions that included the Federal Minister of Transport, Datu Abdul Ghani Gilong, and Tun Fuad Stephens. Islamic conversion among influential persons was an important method for encouraging mass conversions. This can be linked to Rooney's analysis of how the Christian faith was spread among the indigenous communities in North Borneo. Rooney suggested that the conversion of a socially prominent person such as the chief *bobohizan* (native Kadazan-Dusun priestess) in Kuala Penyu tended to influence others, who identified with such persons, to follow suit (Rooney 1981).

USIA was able to employ a similar strategy with the Islamic conversion of prominent politicians in Sabah. The President of USIA from 1968 until 2004, Datuk Haji A.G. Sahari, claims that in the early 1970s, their *Dakwah* movement also used similar methods in persuading indigenous communities to embrace Islam.[3] These involved visiting remote villages in Sabah to spread the Islamic faith as a way of life. He claimed that when a *Ketua Kampung* (village headman) accepted the faith, the whole village would follow suit. From 1970 until June 1977, USIA claimed to have converted 72,390 Kadazan-Dusun, 14,772 Murut, 6,020 Chinese, and 300 others to the Islamic faith — a total of 93,482 new converts.[4] The high-handed manner in which Tun Mustapha marginalized Christian missionary workers was also instrumental to the Islamic conversions of these village communities. Rooney (1981) argued that as a result of the expulsion of Christian missionary workers from these remote villages, the loss of catechist support among rural Christians enabled USIA to intensify its *Dakwah* movement on these villagers.

The ever-increasing activities of USIA prompted the establishment of a proper Islamic council to provide for the welfare needs of the increasing number of Muslim converts. According to Datuk Sahari, USIA originally proposed the formation of an Islamic Council, but it was the newly-elected BERJAYA Government that legally institutionalized the *Majlis Ugama Islam Sabah* (MUIS) in 1977. He claims that this gave BERJAYA the power to undermine the Islamic leadership of USIA.[5] USIA seemed to have been effective in complementing the objectives of USNO in maintaining a substantial political influence in predominantly Muslim areas. BERJAYA, therefore, aimed to institutionalize a religious proxy that would serve to expand its Muslim support base through the establishment of MUIS.

The contest for Islam between MUIS and USIA was evident on many occasions. Without doubt, the BERJAYA Government had the financial capacity to improve the infrastructural needs of the Muslim community.

The BERJAYA Government began pledging a bigger financial allocation for Islamic religious activities, from 6 to 9 million ringgit, including the building of twelve new district mosques in the Third Malaysian Plan.[6] In this way, BERJAYA was able to increase the role of the government in shaping the organizational functions of MUIS. When the State Government and MUIS were not consulted about an important Islamic conference held in Sabah in 1977,[7] BERJAYA became outraged not only because USIA had established a firm alliance with PERKIM, a revered Islamic body at the national level, but also because this incident tended to reflect poorly on the official status of MUIS.[8]

This incident was also a reminder of the factional divisions in BN at the time. PERKIM and its President, Tunku Abdul Rahman, belonged to the pro-USNO faction within BN. The enduring relationship between Tun Mustapha and Tunku Abdul Rahman, and the success of USIA in establishing a national partnership with PERKIM demonstrated the significance of Islamic organization in mobilizing political support for Tun Mustapha. Against this backdrop, it was undeniable that the Islamic *Dakwah* was being used as a 'proxy' for political contests both at the State and Federal levels, which explained why BERJAYA was keen to discredit the Islamic credentials of the leaders of USIA and PERKIM. The BERJAYA Information Chief, Haji Halik Zaman, 'revealed' that Tun Mustapha, President of USIA, was "an active member of a world-wide Jewish Front Organization — The Freemasons".[9] He also accused the Vice President of PERKIM, Tan Sri Abdul Aziz bin Zain, of being part of the organization. The 'holy' alliance between USIA and PERKIM and their alleged involvement in Freemasonry prompted BERJAYA Youth to urge the State Government to bring up the case before the Federal authorities.[10] Tunku Abdul Rahman, claiming that it was an attempt to discredit PERKIM leaders and to take over power in PERKIM, refuted this allegation and, not long after that, Mustapha was appointed Deputy President of PERKIM.[11]

With Islamic revivalism prevailing in the late 1970s, an increasing number of Islamic groups began to espouse Islamic ideals, as well as to propagate doctrines of a 'pure' Islamic way of life. The *Dakwah* movement during this period paid particular attention to the evaluation of the role of Islam in transforming the socio-political and cultural mores of Malaysian society. *Dakwah Islamiah* was especially critical of the process of secularism and viewed the separation of knowledge from religion as un-Islamic (Ismail Haji Ibrahim 1981).[12]

In conceptualizing Islam as *ad-Din*, *Dakwah Islamiah* aimed to revive the moral sanctity of Islam as the religion that upheld a 'purer' life-world against the threats of other religions in Malaysia, as well as the rising permissiveness of modern society. Dr Ismail (Dean of Islamic Studies at Universiti Kebangsaan Malaysia) specifically argues that the other religions in Malaysia were threatening the development of Islam. He further argues that these other religions could 'poison' the minds of Muslims who did not possess a strong belief in Islam (Ismail Haji Ibrahim 1981). William Roff (1998) had charted the process of Islamization, beginning in the late nineteenth century, in Malaya and argued that the judicial practices of the Colonial Administration actually created two autonomous zones of legal development: the civil court and the 'Muhammadan' laws under State Councils which structured its own Islamic judicial bureaucracy, underlining much of Islamic institutional restructuring over the twentieth century. In his study of Islamic law reform in Malaysia, Donald Horowitz claimed that much of the development of Islamic law in the modern period was considerably undertaken by secular lawyers and judges involving the legalization of Islam, instead of the Islamization of the law. This process tended to favour the recruitment of lawyers and judges with a secular legal background, and the incorporation of common law courts, resulting in a "hybridization, borrowing and convergence" of the Malaysian Islamic law (Horowitz 1994, p. 267).

The sociological explanations for the Islamic resurgence discussed by Judith Nagata (1984), Chandra Muzaffar (1987), and Hussin Mutalib (1991) had raised issues of shifting parameters in Malay identity in response to the process of modernization and the global trends of the Islamic Revolutions. On party competition along Islamic lines in West Malaysia, Funston (1980) and Camroux (1996) had documented the extent to which the secular ruling coalition adopted the reformist policies of Islamic laws to limit the scope of other social and political organizations in mobilizing the social forces of Islamization.

In his discussion of the NEP and the economic origins of Malay nationalism, Shamsul (1997) identified the growing disparities between the 'new Malay' middle class and the Malay working class, underlining the cultural predicament of the new Malay dilemma. He argued that Mahathir's vision of creating technocratic and industrialist Malays, becoming major players in the international corporate scene, had led to the introduction of education policies which resulted in the unintended consequence of undermining Malay cultural values. The bifurcation of the middle-class Malays and the 'new Malay' proletariat was gradually reflected in the growing lifestyle and economic differences between these groups, which could potentially radicalize the poor into questioning the moral grounds of the Federal Government's policies, and hence the Islamic credibility of UMNO. In this context, UMNO began to view Islam as a potent social force to radicalize the 'new Malay' proletariat, providing rich grounds for organizations such as ABIM and PAS to mobilize their support. In overcoming the competing politics of Islam, Mahathir succeeded in poaching Anwar Ibrahim from ABIM, who became influential in initiating Islamic reforms within its internal politics and moving towards institutionalizing Islamic values within the national government's administration.[13] The other significant step undertaken by UMNO was the extensive Federal backing given in the jurisdictional expansion of *Syariah* reform, as well as the corporate financial support provided for the Muslim community in the form of Islamic banking, insurance and property management (Hamayotsu 2003). Creating institutional support for the Muslim community was an important strategy for UMNO to prove its Islamic credentials against PAS. These developments could have pressured or inspired BERJAYA to emulate them in overcoming the 'holy' alliance between USIA and PERKIM, and ultimately replacing USNO's Islamic influence in Sabah.

In order to counter the elements of political militancy among the growing number of Islamic groups, the Federal and State Governments alike strengthened their commitment to the administration of Islam through proper religious institutions. The Malaysian Government therefore took over the official sponsorship of 'correct' *Dakwah* organizations and also scrutinized other non-official *Dakwah* movements, in order to ensure that they followed the official guidelines. The national alliance between USIA and PERKIM prompted the BERJAYA Government to adopt the Federal Government's policy in intensifying the propagation of Islam in Sabah. The 1976 Federal Constitution amendment added a provision to the Constitution of the State of Sabah, giving power to the *Yang di-Pertuan Agong* as the Head of the Muslim Religion in Sabah State. Originally, the *Yang di Pertuan Negeri* was the Head of Islam in Sabah, and the Sabah Constitution did not confine the position to a Muslim only. The 1976 amendment effectively put an end to the possibility of a non-Muslim becoming the Head of State. The Administration of Muslim Law Enactment 1977 was introduced to make the administration of Muslim law in Sabah analogous to the system in the States of Peninsular Malaysia (Ahmad Ibrahim 1978). The Sabah State Assembly approved the Muslim Law Enactment Bill for the purpose of tightening the administration of Muslim law and to include additional punishable offences such as *khalwat*, or illicit proximity.[14] By this token, Harris promised to extend "whatever aid necessary by MUIS in the propagation of the Islamic religion".[15]

CONVERSION CEREMONIES

With BERJAYA's support, MUIS was able to intensify its *Dakwah* activities in the early 1980s. Conversion ceremonies were featured widely in the media and the BERJAYA Government regularly included the message of Islamic propagation in the daily newspaper to reflect their seriousness about Islamic reforms within the government's administration. As soon as MUIS was established, BERJAYA attributed the importance of *Dakwah* to "developing the Islamic religion in the State", and even Muslim students were urged to propagate Islam.[16] In the context of developing the Islamic religion in Sabah, this effort was particularly targeted at the pagan population in the interior regions.[17]

USIA had been carrying out *Dakwah* activities in remote areas since the 1960s; however, its Islamization activities could not match the intensity of those of MUIS. The Islamization policy of MUIS served BERJAYA's aim of increasing the number of Muslim supporters for the party. Since a considerable size of the pagan population in the interior were strong BERJAYA supporters, they therefore became important targets of BERJAYA's Islamization policy. In 1978, MUIS received a total of 350,000 ringgit in Federal funding for religious development projects in rural areas; the committee of the catechist Parish Councils in Kota Kinabalu and Keningau received about one-sixth (70,000 ringgit) of the total Federal budget (420,000 ringgit) reserved for this purpose (Sabah 1980).

Conversion ceremonies were featured widely in the media in the early 1980s, with high-ranking public officials being witnesses to these events. Table 6.1 catalogues some of these ceremonies. These mass conversion ceremonies were carried out in the interior heartlands of the Kadazan-Dusun and Murut, and at the northern tip of Sabah, where the Rungus population were the dominant ethnic group. Villages in the district of Ranau and, particularly, Kundasang had been important targets of Islamic conversions by USIA since the 1960s. The Federal Minister under USNO, Ghani Gilong, was a prominent politician in Kundasang who embraced Islam in the 1960s. One prominent farmer in Kundasang related his experience of a mass conversion under USNO and of how the Dusun communities had their 'last supper' of the 'forbidden meat' before they embraced Islam the next day.[18]

In 1984, MUIS disclosed that a total of 23,500 people in Sabah had embraced Islam since its establishment on 16 February 1977.[19] As a follow-up to their new faith, missionary training centres were built for the new converts to intensify their understanding of the Islamic faith, as well as to help them embrace the Islamic way of life. *Pusat Latihan Dakwah Keningau*

Table 6.1
Selected Mass Conversions in Sabah, 1981–84

Date	Town	Ethnicity of converts	Number of converts	Witnesses
05/07/80	Keningau	Murut	900	Suffian Koroh (State Minister); Mahathir Mohamad
11/07/81	Labuk Sugut	Dusun Sungei	183	Harris Salleh
30/08/82	Tambunan	Kadazan	775	Mahathir Mohamad
30/08/82	Kundasang	Dusun	425	Mahathir Mohamad
02/10/82	Kundasang	Dusun	200	Yang di-Pertuan Agong
21/01/83	Kg. Magindai	Rungus	320	Anwar Ibrahim
22/01/83	Kg. Bongkol	Rungus	312	Anwar Ibrahim
16/04/83	Kota Marudu	Rungus	2,000	Tuan yang Terutama Adnan Robert; Iraqi and Kuwaiti Ambassadors to Malaysia
18/04/83	Tenom	Murut	155	Harris Salleh; Saudi Businessman; the Mufti of Brunei
07/06/83	Nunuk Ragang and Kg. Sinarut (Ranau)	Dusun	190	Sanusi Junid (Fed. Minister of National and Rural Development); Harris Salleh; Mohd Noor Mansoor; Indonesian Consul Budi Ismardi

Source: Reports in *Kemajuan* magazine and the *Daily Express* newspaper.

and *Pusat Latihan Dakwah Tongod* were both set up in 1979 for the purpose of strengthening the Islamic faith of the new converts. Both these centres were located in the interior heartlands of the Kadazan-Dusun and Murut population. *Pusat Latihan Dakwah Sikuati* was built in 1979 and was located among the predominantly Rungus population in the district of Kudat and the Bengkoka Peninsula in Northern Sabah. These missionary centres were administered by MUIS until 1984, when BERJAYA proposed to the Federal Government to federalize MUIS and take control of the administration of Islamic affairs in Sabah.[20]

The mass conversion of the predominantly pagan population in Sabah was based on two assumptions. Firstly, that they did not possess an official religion, and in this context, MUIS saw it as its duty to propagate Islam among the pagan community. Secondly, by targeting the pagan population, MUIS was less likely to run the risk of antagonizing the Christian community in Sabah. Through MUIS, the *Dakwah* movement, the BERJAYA party was able to transform and manufacture the political support of the pagan community into Muslim-based support. The presence of Federal ministers and politicians at all these rituals of Islamic conversion represented a symbolic process where Islam became politically salient in the relations of power and patronage between the state and its subjects.

BERJAYA's use of the media to effectively portray its Islamization policy also served the aims of the Federal Government in creating a greater Muslim nation within Malaysia. Anthony Smith (1999, p. 193) argued that regime changes often lead to the need for "rulers to legitimate their position through attempts to homogenize their populations. Such attempts include linguistic standardization and/or conversion, as with the example of Russification under the last Tsar". Islam therefore became a means to 'homogenize' or at least to categorize the complexity of Sabah's native communities into relatively more manageable groups of Muslim and non-Muslim *bumiputera.*

Harrison argued that Islamic influence in Borneo could be traced before 1500 owing to discovery of Jawi text in the Idahan language (Harrison 1973). Islam therefore had impacted upon the native population for a long time, but Harrison ruled out the inference of mass conversion or immigration and believed conversions were carried out on a small-scale basis by religious teachers. The 1960 North Borneo census shows that the Muslim population comprised about one-third of the Sabah population but their numbers grew only in accordance with natural increase, for missionary work by Muslims was limited (British North Borneo 1961). Since the Kadazan-Dusun and Murut communities tended to live in the interior regions of Sabah, Islamic influence was limited to the coastal areas.

The Christian faith, on the other hand, became the dominant religion of the Kadazan-Dusun, Murut and Chinese populations, especially after the BNBC established itself in the late nineteenth century. The majority of both the Kadazan-Dusun and Murut were pagans but the number of Christian converts among them increased about 65 per cent in the space of ten years. The total number of Christians in 1960 was 46,155 — an increase of

30,000 converts since 1951. The first Christian missionary arrived in 1859 but the expansion of the BNBC Administration facilitated the spread of Christianity in the interior regions. The work of the Christian churches also included the teaching of English and elementary education with basic medical provisions. Overall secondary school student enrolment in North Borneo was 54 per cent in missionary schools, 22.5 per cent in government schools and 23.5 per cent in Chinese schools (North Borneo 1960). Christian missionary schools therefore seemed to acquire wider regard among the non-Muslim population for post-primary education.

Writing during the colonial period, when Christian missionaries were common in North Borneo, Monica Glyn-Jones (1953) argued that Christianity was introduced in ways which were compatible with the belief system of the pagan communities, in particular the concept of creation and protection that the Kadazan-Dusun people already understood.[21] The Dusunic peoples observed the similarities between their oral histories and the Biblical narratives of the Old Testament, especially in relation to the redemptive analogies of the Christian Messiah (Pugh-Kitingan 1989, p. 385). As *Kinoiringan* was replaced with the concept of God, certain *adat* rituals may have become archaic or were practised in different ways, although the more important social events, such as the *Kaamatan* (Harvest Festival), still retained their traditional practices, which were still widely revered by the Christian natives.

It is understandable that the new Christian converts had to abandon some of their pagan beliefs and practices. However, the Kadazan-Dusun sense of identity and their everyday lives were held together by the practices of *adat* — the social and legal customs of the Kadazan-Dusun community (Blood 1990). The Murut communities, on the other hand, had different linguistic and ethnic backgrounds from the Kadazan-Dusun but they had their own established forms of law and customs that sustained certain elements of traditional structure within their social organizations (Blood 1990; Brewis 1990; Harris 1990). As a faith, Christianity became the nominal religion of the Kadazan-Dusun and Murut communities, but the local customs and *adat* — for the Kadazan-Dusun people — still retained their practicalities in everyday social life, especially among communities at the village level. As *adat* remained an important aspect of social interaction and custom within Kadazan-Dusun society, the introduction of Islamic laws and strict rituals into the lives of the new Muslim converts could have generated certain unexpected changes in their lives. These became apparent in the conflicting values between *adat* and Islamic rules in regulating the practicalities of family inheritance, marriage, funeral rites, and the consumption of food and drinks.

IMMIGRATION AND THE NAME GAME

In the second half of the BERJAYA Administration, the growing number of new Muslim converts, together with the influx of Muslims from the Philippines and Indonesia, contributed to the overall increase in the Muslim population in Sabah. Under the USNO regime, Sabah became the training ground for the Moro paramilitary troops and the strategic point for the supply of weapons from other Muslim nations to be smuggled into the Southern Philippines (McKenna 1998, pp. 148–57). In the 1972 civil war in the Southern Philippines, around one million people were internally displaced and more than 100,000 people fled to nearby Malaysia (Paridah Abd. Samad and Darulsalam Abu Bakar 1992).

In 1970, the Filipino population in Sabah was officially 20,367, or about 3 per cent of the total population (Sabah 1971). This increased to 92,000 in 1978, although unofficially the figure was estimated at 140,000, or about 15 per cent of Sabah's population, settled mainly in Tawau, Sandakan, Lahad Datu and Semporna.[22] By 1989, the Filipino population in Sabah was estimated to have risen to 350,000, or 26.9 per cent of the total population of 1.3 million in Sabah.[23] With the ongoing conflict in the Southern Philippines, the influx of illegal Filipino immigrants into Sabah continued even after the 1976 peace pact. In contrast to the national policies on stemming the flow of (non-Muslim) Vietnamese refugees into Peninsular Malaysia, the Home Minister, Ghazali Shafie, did not impose a similar policy upon the Filipino refugees in Sabah.

In defending the policy to confer refugee status on Filipino immigrants, the Home Minister justified that "their presence will not have adverse effects on the peace and order of the country because they intended to go back" whereas the "presence of the Vietnamese immigrants could have adverse consequences on the country as they had no intention of returning to their homeland after the war".[24] Mahathir also supported this, saying that "there would be social disruption if the (Vietnamese) refugees got off the islands and blended with the local people", and that Malaysia might have to "arm itself with legislation to shoo the (Vietnamese) refugees if necessary".[25]

The open door policy to Muslim refugees — although strongly denied by the Home Minister — was sustained by the BERJAYA Government partly because of humanitarian concerns, but it also conveniently provided a ready source of cheap labour in Sabah. Filipino immigration aside, a considerable number of Indonesian workers were also absorbed into the Malaysian labour force at the same time. In the period 1971–80, Sabah experienced a higher rate of population growth, at 5.3 per cent per annum, compared to that of

Peninsular Malaysia, at 2.6 per cent, or Sarawak, at 3 per cent per annum (Malaysia 1981). The growth of the labour force in Sabah, at 5.1 per cent per annum during the period 1971–80, was also higher than the growth rates estimated for Peninsular Malaysia and Sarawak, mainly due to these two factors.

Until 1974, there were tight measures in monitoring their entry into Sabah; however, these were dropped in a move to make their entry easier.[26] The registration of Filipinos started again in 1977; however, this was only conducted on a voluntary basis. The Federal budget for the maintenance of housing for the Filipino refugees in Sabah was 252,450 ringgit for the year 1978.[27] However, due to the confidentiality of such information, the author could only speculate that most of these Filipino refugees settled and the process of naturalization allowed them to remain in Sabah indefinitely.

The presence of Filipinos and Indonesians added a new dimension to the ongoing Islamic reforms being undertaken by the BERJAYA Government. These Filipino Muslim refugees became instrumental to the political goals of the BERJAYA Government. Harris remarked that, "Muslims are multiplying faster and some of the refugees will become voters. In five years Muslims will hold the balance and Muslims will form the government".[28] In the official declaration of a new village for Filipino refugees in Kampung Bahagia in Sandakan, Harris described how the great majority of these refugees in Sabah were law-abiding and praised their willingness to take up jobs that local people were unwilling to perform, stating further that they were "of the same stock as the Malaysian people and therefore would not be difficult to assimilate".[29]

'*Pribumi*' became the umbrella term encompassing the refugees and the twenty-four different indigenous ethnic groups in the 1982 census. The BERJAYA Government explained that the term '*pribumi*' had the blessing of the Federal Government, to facilitate the process of achieving greater unity among the diverse indigenous ethnic communities in Sabah.[30] In the 1980 population census, the Sabah population was divided into '*pribumi*', which stood at 83 per cent, with a remainder of 16 per cent Chinese and 1 per cent 'others'. The 1980 census showed that the percentage of Muslims in the population in Sabah was 51 per cent — an increase of 11 per cent from 40 per cent in the 1970 census. The '*pribumi*' tag had the effect of homogenizing the indigenous identity in Sabah and, in the context of Islamization, the identity of the *Pribumi* was more likely to be linked to Islam than the other religions in Sabah. Tables 6.2 and 6.3 compare the 1970 and 1980 census reports respectively, showing a sharp increase of 11 per cent in the Muslim population with the deliberate use of the term '*pribumi*' to

Table 6.2
Religious Distribution by Ethnic Group, 1970

	Kadazan	Murut	Bajau	Malay	Other *bumiputera*	Chinese	Indonesian	Others	Total
Islam	3%	0%	11%	3%	14%	0%	6%	3%	40%
Christian	13%	2%	0%	0%	2%	5%	0%	1%	24%
Buddhist	0%	0%	0%	0%	0%	9%	0%	0%	10%
No religion	6%	1%	0%	0%	2%	2%	0%	0%	12%
Others	6%	1%	0%	0%	1%	5%	0%	1%	15%
Total	28%	5%	12%	3%	19%	21%	6%	6%	100%

Source: Report of the 1970 Population and Housing Census.

Table 6.3
Religious Distribution by Ethnic Group, 1980

	Pribumi	Chinese	Other	Total
Islam	51%	0%	0%	51%
Christian	23%	4%	0%	27%
Buddhist	0%	8%	0%	8%
No religion	5%	1%	0%	6%
Other	2%	3%	0%	7%
Total	83%	16%	1%	100%

Source: Report of the 1980 Population and Housing Census, Sabah.

simplify the ethnic diversity and to accentuate the relatively higher number of Muslims in Sabah.

THE DISPUTE OVER *KAAMATAN*

In his 1982 *Kaamatan* speech, the King supported Islamic missionary movements in Sabah by emphasizing the need for the government to fulfil the spiritual development of the people in Sabah.[31] In Keningau, the royal couple witnessed the mass Islamic conversion of 326 adults and 112 children from Nabawan and Tenom. The royal entourage continued their tour of 'spiritual blessing' during the Harvest Festival and witnessed mass conversion ceremonies in Kundasang, Sandakan and Labuan. Since the 1960s, *Kaamatan* had officially become an important ceremonial event celebrating the cultural life of the Kadazan-Dusun ethnic communities. The presence of the King to promote Islam during *Kaamatan* in Sabah was not well received among the Kadazan-Dusun communities. *Kaamatan* is a vital cultural tradition in the *adat* of thanksgiving, whereby a group of female priestesses (*bobohizan*) perform a traditional thanksgiving ritual to the spirit of the rice for a good harvest. The presence of the King was generally perceived as displacing the role of the *bobohizan*, turning the 1982 *Kaamatan* into a royal seal of approval symbolizing Federal Government support for BERJAYA's leadership in Islam.

A senior Christian Kadazan BERJAYA minister defended the event by arguing that the "Harvest is no longer a Kadazan festival".[32] The '*Pribumi*' move and the State-sponsored *Kaamatan* reflected BERJAYA's ambition to espouse the National Culture Policy of the Federal Government. Pugh-

Kitingan contended that, as the National Culture Policy was designed to protect the rights of the Malay majority in Peninsular Malaysia, it was therefore incompatible with the complex nature of the culturally diverse ethnic societies in Sabah (Pugh-Kitingan 1989). One of the cultural implications of such a policy affected the public consumption of *tapai* (rice wine) when it was discouraged by a State-level organizing committee.[33] The prohibition of the public consumption of alcohol reflected the Islamic undertone of BERJAYA.

The Islamic emphasis of the *Kaamatan* in Keningau prompted the President of the Sabah Kadazan Cultural Association, Pairin Kitingan, who was also a BERJAYA minister, to hold another *Kaamatan* in Tambunan. This came as a response to requests from several districts that were not able to participate in the Keningau Festival.[34] Pairin's endeavour was criticized by BERJAYA. In an official statement, non-Muslim BERJAYA officials accused Pairin of insulting the King and BERJAYA subsequently denied public funding and amenities to support the function.[35] Despite official criticism, the Tambunan Festival was attended by about ten thousand people, who came from as far away as Sandakan, Tawau, and Lahad Datu, and the role of the *bobohizan* was reinstated in the celebration.[36] When Pairin resigned, Harris said that it was due to the "plans and wishes" of the BERJAYA leaders, in order to make way for younger leaders.[37]

The *Kaamatan* became a contested issue and caused a rift between the State Government and the Sabah Kadazan Cultural Association (SKCA) when the latter organized the second celebration. Within the Sabah Kadazan Cultural Association there was also division among its leadership and its members over this issue. There was the State Government camp and the Pairin supporters, camp within the SKCA, and the whole issue of cultural representation became embroiled within the wider political discourse. Conrad Mojuntin accused the heads of cultural associations of spreading rumours among villagers that the State Government was out to destroy their culture and suggested the resignation of all politicians holding posts in cultural associations. These associations included the Sabah Kadazan Cultural Association, the United Sabah Dusun Association (USDA), the *Persatuan Sabah Bajau Bersatu* (PSBB, United Sabah Bajau Association), and the *Persatuan Brunei Bumiputera Sabah* (PBBS, Sabah Brunei *Bumiputera* Association).[38]

THE BERJAYA END GAME

BERJAYA's second term witnessed a host of leaders being expelled from the party on the grounds of creating "disunity and ill feelings" within the party.[39] State Finance Minister Mohd Noor justified these expulsions on the basis of a 'modified democracy' chosen by the people, whereby the freedom of speech and actions were governed by the BERJAYA party's regulations, constitutions and other guidelines.[40] A by-election in Pairin's constituency of Tambunan was declared for 29 December 1984. In the run up to the by-election, Harris issued press statements informing the village heads in Tambunan that, "Only the government can give you development, progress and prosperity. Opposition means nothing but trouble."[41] Harris also warned the village heads from Keningau and Tenom that they would have to vacate their positions if any of them opposed the government.[42]

In defending against accusations of religious intolerance, Pairin stated that, "The people of Tambunan were not against Islam as the official religion but only coercion of certain people into embracing the religion."[43] As an independent candidate in the Tambunan by-election, Pairin won 3,685 votes against the BERJAYA candidate, Roger Ongkili, who only managed 637 votes. The defeat prompted a BERJAYA minister to remark that, "This means that the Independent candidate and his supporters will be given the opportunity of looking after the people here without BERJAYA government help."[44] As of 1 January 1985, the Sabah Government abolished Tambunan's status as a separate district and placed Tambunan under the Keningau District Office. The District Officer, the Native Chiefs and the village heads lost their jobs, and all government aid was withdrawn.[45] Pairin's protest against the withdrawal of development funding was met with BERJAYA's accusation that he also took part in the collective decision supporting tough measures against USNO supporters in Usukan, Kunak and Semporna.[46] Mohd Noor defended the policy on Tambunan thus: "It was BERJAYA's political right in the political process."[47]

BERJAYA's developmentalist approach to Tambunan underlined the political strategies employed by the BN Government in punishing opposition strongholds in the Peninsula. Suffian Koroh gave examples of how the BN Government put a stop to all development projects in Kelantan and how UMNO fired some 800 village headmen suspected of being PAS supporters.[48] In mid-January 1985, seventeen village headmen were sacked and the Tambunan Native Court came under the authority of the Keningau Native Court. Harris justified the government's action by saying that "These village leaders were political appointees and they would be dismissed if they were no good and be replaced when we could find suitable people."[49]

Pairin's new party, the *Parti Bersatu Sabah* (PBS), was registered on 5 March 1985, and this was immediately followed by the dissolution of the Sabah State Legislative Assembly on 18 March. In a show of support for

BERJAYA, Mahathir declared that the Federal Government "will sink or swim with BERJAYA".[50]

At the national level, Pairin was portrayed as politicizing the issue of religion, being a threat to "national security" and was accused of scheming on the plot to secede Sabah from Malaysia.[51] Citing high prospects of treason, Federal Minister Kadir Shiekh Fadzir urged the police to monitor all the meetings and activities of the opposition parties and to record all their statements.[52] In Sabah, the BERJAYA party tried to discredit Pairin by accusing him of using the people of Tambunan to obtain agricultural land for his own benefit, and said that Pairin was ungrateful as the recipient of 500,000 ringgit under BERJAYA's ABC system.[53]

We have seen that BERJAYA's Islamization drive increasingly undermined its claim to stand for 'multiracial' politics. The BERJAYA leaders tried to resuscitate its 'multiracial' appeal before the 1985 Sabah election but to no avail. These efforts included differential financial rewards targeting the *Pribumi* and the Chinese business communities. The BERJAYA Government announced that, "Every Pribumi in Sabah over the age of 21 is an indirect shareholder of about 20 companies operated by the Yayasan Pribumi Sabah (YPS)".[54] The announcement was followed by the YPS' purchase of *Amanah Saham Nasional* shares for about 360,000 *pribumis*, totalling 56 million ringgit. Harris also allocated 18 million ringgit annually to MUIS for its missionary activities and the development of Islam in Sabah.[55] In an effort to target the business community, the BERJAYA Government proposed the reduction of licence fees and rentals of up to 66 per cent, going back to 1 January 1985.[56]

In the 1985 State election, the PBS won 25 seats,[57] USNO clinched 16 seats, BERJAYA had 6 seats, and Pasok won 1 seat. BERJAYA won 4 seats in Muslim-majority areas and 2 seats in the Chinese-dominated constituencies. The Chinese votes seemed equally split between PBS and BERJAYA, but that did not take into account Chinese who had been strong supporters of DAP in Sandakan.[58] Whilst the Kadazan-Dusun and Murut votes seemed to form the bastion of PBS support, most of the Muslim votes went back to USNO.

Mavis Puthucheary (1985) argued that in the 1985 State election, the results showed no party could claim exclusive representation of any particular religious or ethnic group. Whilst there was broader support for PBS as a party, local personalities and issues tended to influence the people's support for USNO or BERJAYA. BERJAYA had 31 per cent of the total votes cast in the 17 Muslim-dominated constituencies, whereas USNO obtained 42 per cent. Puthucheary provided three reasons explaining the shift in the Muslim vote to USNO: firstly, USNO had stronger roots within the Muslims in Sabah, regardless of the nature of the support from the Federal Government; secondly, the loss of support for USNO in the 1980s was due to a leadership crisis within the party; and, thirdly, BERJAYA was instrumental in USNO's expulsion from the BN in 1984.

The Islamic resurgence in Malaysia had significant bearing upon Sabah politics under BERJAYA. BERJAYA's strategy in adopting the Islamization policies and reforms initiated by UMNO effectively resulted in the extension of Islamic jurisdiction in Sabah, and therefore strengthened the institutional role of Islam far better than what USNO could have achieved under Tun Mustapha. However, this process went against the 'multiracial' ideology of BERJAYA, and even became a source of divisiveness within Muslim communities as a result of BERJAYA's selective developmental strategy against supporters of the opposition party, USNO. The mass Islamic conversions, the use of the term '*pribumi*' to mask the inclusion of Muslim refugees in the 1980 Sabah census, and the 1982 *Kaamatan* incident contributed to the cultural marginalization of non-Muslim ethnic groups in Sabah. These events not only brought back the painful memory of the political marginalization of the Kadazan-Dusun leaders during the Sabah Alliance crises, but also highlighted the fact that BERJAYA had effectively instituted Islamic governance in Sabah. Despite BERJAYA's policies of Islamization and Islamic reforms, it was obvious that BERJAYA had used Islam to undermine USNO's political influence among the Muslim community in Sabah. The selective developmental approach against opposition strongholds in both Muslim and non-Muslim areas showed the extent to which BERJAYA's developmental priorities were narrowly defined along lines of party support. Islam was used as a way of gaining political goodwill within the BN, and to close ranks with UMNO in particular. No party could claim exclusive representation of any particular religious or ethnic group and, particularly for BERJAYA, it had not really developed strong roots among the Muslim community, nor had it identified with the non-Muslim communities in Sabah. BERJAYA's decision to focus on the strategy of strengthening Federal-State relations at the administrative and party level contributed to its failure to develop strong social relations that the local population in Sabah could identify with. BERJAYA's effort to mobilize support from the political elites in Kuala Lumpur to strengthen its political standing resulted in their own failure to increase their knowledge and understanding of the local setting, which ultimately affected BERJAYA's ability to implement policies that really addressed the needs of the local population.

CONCLUSION

Under USNO, the State Government in Sabah fervently promoted Islamization largely as a means of securing, or attempting to secure, political loyalty primarily through *cultural* claims and an expanded concept of Malayness (Tilman 1976). Under BERJAYA, however, the politics of Islamization and ethnicity became entwined with a *developmentalist* vision, producing a curiously hybrid administration that, on the one hand, promoted technocratic solutions to Sabah's economic woes, but, on the other hand, tied this in practice to the preferential treatment of Muslims and Muslims communities.

Thus far, BERJAYA pursued a dual strategy of political control in Sabah, matching an Islamization drive that sought to homogenize the population with party-oriented developmentalism. Hence, in the attempt to gain Islamic leadership credibility and legitimacy, BERJAYA failed to live up to its multiracial pledges. BERJAYA's policies on development, immigration and culture led to crises of leadership within the party, prompting an exodus of leaders who had become disillusioned with BERJAYA. In the end, BERJAYA's pro-Federal Islamic policies eventually led to its own downfall in the 1985 State election. The biggest communities to shift away from supporting BERJAYA were the Kadazan-Dusun and the Chinese communities — BERJAYA's original supporters in the 1976 State election. Prior to the 1985 election, the BERJAYA Government had intensified its developmentalist strategy, that is, regulating government developments according to party support — a familiar tactic that was used against the Sandakan and USNO constituencies. Such tactics had been known to primarily target the authority of the office bearer at district levels. The abrogation of Tambunan from the status of a district and the unprecedented transfer of senior government officials in Sandakan epitomized the extent to which BERJAYA tried to regulate development by manipulating authority at the local or district administrative levels.

Towards the end of BERJAYA's rule, the polemic of Islamic leadership gradually shaped the landscape of Sabah politics. The rise of PBS and its denunciation of mass Islamization saw the coming of age of a new brand of politics which underlined the significance of identity in political expression and representation. The political comeback of USNO, on the other hand, reflected a growing demand for Islam to play a greater political role in Sabah politics. Sabah politics then diverged into two broad representations: one that emphasized the salience of cultural identity, and the other that stressed the importance of Islam. In effect, BERJAYA had successfully created a political climate where new lines were being drawn according to the religious categories of Muslim *bumiputera* and non-Muslim *bumiputera*. The BERJAYA Government's actions in Sabah therefore serves to elucidate the tension between the political control of the State/Government and the political legitimacy it could garner from the people. This tension becomes even more problematic in multi-ethnic and multi-religious societies, where the State or Government may seek to resolve this puzzle through the prioritization of one group's development over others, but this is itself a dangerous path to tread.

Notes

1 These constituencies were: Kudat, Likas, Kota Kinabalu, Elopura, Sandakan, Karamunting, Tenom and Bandar Tawau.

2 *Far Eastern Economic Review*, 27 March 1971; Ibid., 4 March 1974.

3 Datuk Haji A.G. Sahari, interview by the author, Kota Kinabalu, March 2003.

4 A.G. Sahari, interview by the author.

5 Datuk Haji A.G. Sahari, interview by the author, Kota Kinabalu, 15 June 2003.

6 *Daily Express*, 1 March 1977.

7 The Islamic conference was jointly organized by USIA and the *Pertubuhan Kebajikan Islam Malaysia* (PERKIM).

8 *Daily Express*, 11 February 1977; Ibid., 12 February 1977; Ibid., 22 February 1977.

9 Ibid., 4 March 1977.

10 Ibid., 7 March 1977.

11 *Kinabalu Sabah Times*, 6 August 1977.

12 "Kita tidak boleh mengharapkan kewujudan iman ini di dalam semua anggota masyarakat kita, kerana kita telah beratus-ratus tahun dipesongkan dari ajaran Islam dalam konsepnya yang menyeluruh itu, kita dididik, dan diasuh dalam sistem pelajaran dan social yang memisahkan ilmu agama dari ilmu-ilmu lain, memisahkan agama dari sistem hidup seharian dan urusan-urusan keduniaan yang dikatakan tidak ada hubungannya dengan agama" (Ismail Hj. Ibrahim 1981, p. 44).

13 *Daily Express*, 20 January 1983.

14 Ibid., 19 December 1979.

15 Ibid., 19 September 1977.

16 Ibid., 27 July 1978.

17 Ibid., 20 January 1983.

18 Interview with a former *Ketua Kampung* in the Kundasang area, Kundasang, 25 May 2003.

19 *Daily Express*, 18 July 1984.

20 Ibid., 22 May 1984.

21 "The concept of Kinoiringan as the supreme god of the Dusun people had a similar concept of God's creation and the genesis of life in Christianity. Hence Kinoiringan was easily recognized as God the Father, and His Son was not Tawadakon the mischief-maker but Jesus Christ the Savior of Mankind."

22 *Far Eastern Economic Review*, 12 May 1978.

23 Ibid., 16 March 1989.

24 *Daily Express*, 24 November 1979.

25 Ibid., 24 November 1979; *Far Eastern Economic Review*, 14 July 1983.

26 *Study of Resettlement Projects for Displaced Persons in Sabah*, Sabah Government Report, May 1977.

27 *Laporan kemajuan pelaksanaan bagi rancangan perpindahan orang-orang pelarian Filipina di Sabah*, 1978; *Laporan peruntukan negeri dan persekutuan bagi projek-projek kecil luar Bandar, Tahun 1978–1979*, 15 August 1980. It was impossible to compare these figures with other years because the Sabah Archive has classified them as confidential.

28 *Asiaweek*, 7 June 1985.

29 *Daily Express*, 5 December 1983.

30 Ibid., 15 January 1983.

31 Ibid., 11 May 1982.

32 Ibid., 12 June 1984.

33 The drinking of *tapai* performs a social function which brings communities together in many places in Sabah and this activity is culturally significant during the celebration of the Harvest Festival (*Daily Express*, 1 March 1983).

34 *Daily Express*, 12 May 1982.

35 Ibid., 20 May 1982.

36 Ibid., 28 June 1982.

37 Pairin Kitingan resigned from the Ministry of Resource Development, whilst Yap Pak Leong resigned from the Ministry of Town and Country Development. Pairin and Yap still remained assemblymen for Tambunan and Elopura respectively (*Daily Express*, 22 June 1982).

38 *Daily Express*, 5 February 1985.

39 Besides Pairin, Yap Pak Leong, Halik Zaman, Pengiran Othman Rauf, Mohd Dun Banir and Robert Evans were allegedly 'guilty' of criticizing the State Government in the press. The BERJAYA Supreme Souncil decreed that members were not allowed to make any statements to the media about the policies of the State or Federal Governments without the approval of the party (*Daily Express*, 30 March 1983).

40 *Daily Express*, 13 June 1983.

41 Ibid., 31 August 1984.

42 Ibid., 5 September 1984.

43 Ibid., 29 September 1984.

44 Ibid., 31 December 1984.

[45] Ibid., 1 January 1985.

[46] Ibid., 4 January 1985.

[47] Ibid., 9 January 1985.

[48] Ibid., 15 January 1985.

[49] Ibid., 21 January 1985.

[50] Ibid., 5 April 1985.

[51] Ibid., 13 April 1985.

[52] Ibid., 15 April 1985.

[53] Ibid., 19 April 1985.

[54] Ibid., 1 April 1985.

[55] Ibid., 9 April 1985.

[56] This was the reversal of a policy which was implemented in January 1983, affecting the Municipal Councils of Kota Kinabalu, Sandakan, Tawau and Lahad Datu (*Daily Express*, 16 April 1985).

[57] This included a seat in Moyog by a PBS-backed independent candidate.

[58] DAP controlled the Sandakan constituency during the 1978 and 1982 general elections.

7

EPILOGUE AND CONCLUSION

This book has examined the political dynamics of the relationship between ethnic politics and developmentalism in the context of a minority-dominated state on the periphery of a political federation. It has focused attention on a specific period associated with the emergence, rise, and demise of the BERJAYA party in Sabah. It has argued that the BERJAYA period was instrumental in the reshaping of Federal-State relations in Sabah, and that the contours of BERJAYA's political fortunes can best be understood by locating it within the competing pressures of 'bottom-up' demands for political and cultural autonomy and the 'top-down' pressures of a centralizing Federal Government that was suspicious of such demands. The path BERJAYA trod in order to mediate these pressures — jettisoning its initial 'multiracial' stance in favour of a conjunction of Islamization with developmentalist policies, in an attempt to mould a population more conducive to Federal ambitions — had some initial success but eventually generated a sufficiently strong popular backlash that saw the party swept from power in 1985.

This chapter concludes the analysis by tracing political developments in the State in the post-BERJAYA period, demonstrating that such tensions continued to frame the political process in Sabah until the Federal regime changed tack in 1994 by dropping any further support for 'multiracialism' in the State and, instead, imposed a West Malaysia-style ethnic coalition, backed by a concerted developmentalist drive. While ethnic and religious discontent and tensions remain in the State, this formula has effectively neutered Sabah as a site of political contestation.

It is important at the outset to note that in seeking to oust the BERJAYA Government from power in Sabah, Pairin and the PBS did not set themselves up in direct opposition to the BN coalition in Kuala Lumpur, and repeatedly avowed their intention to seek entry to the coalition should they win the election, much as BERJAYA had done when it first ousted USNO. Whereas BERJAYA had had the backing of the Federal Government in its attempt to replace USNO, however, the PBS lacked similar support in 1985 and was refused entry. With only a slim majority in the State Assembly and facing legal challenges from Mustapha and Harris and harassment from Federal agencies, Pairin soon decided that the only viable option was to return to the polls to seek a new, stronger mandate. These elections were held in May 1986, and gave Pairin the decisive victory he sought, winning an absolute majority of the votes cast and two-thirds control of the State Assembly. Faced with such a clear mandate, the Federal Government relented and admitted PBS to the coalition.

The relationship between the PBS and the Federal Government remained strained, however, with the PBS more willing than other BN parties to speak out against Federal Government policies, such as the controversial amendments to the Official Secrets Act in 1986.[1] These tensions were highlighted after the 1987 leadership challenge in UMNO, which gave birth to a splinter party, *Semangat '46* (or Spirit of '46 — a reference to the year that UMNO was founded), which in turn managed to forge a semi-united opposition front to contest the 1990 Federal elections. Before that election, speculation was rife that a number of smaller BN components would leave the coalition if the opposition seemed to be able to form a government. The PBS was one of these parties, but, in any event, Pairin showed his hand before the election, declaring that the PBS was withdrawing from the BN to support the opposition. By making his announcement after nominations for the election had closed, Pairin also denied the BN the chance to field alternative candidates against PBS. Mahathir's bitterness was obvious; it was a "stab in the back", particularly as it came barely forty-eight hours after he had visited Sabah, and been assured by Pairin of his loyalty.[2]

The BN won the Federal election, but with a considerably reduced majority; the PBS retained control of the Sabah State Assembly, which was not part of the election. In response, the BN immediately launched a war of attrition against the rogue state and its PBS Government. Barely a month after the election, one of Pairin's top aides, Dr Maximus Ongkili, was briefly detained without trial for alleged involvement in a secessionist plot. In the following few days, Pairin himself was charged with a minor count of corruption, and a number of other PBS leaders, including Pairin's Deputy Chief Minister, Yong Teck Lee, were arrested for participating in an illegal demonstration prior to the election. Later in the year, Jeffrey Kitingan, Pairin's brother and Head of the State Development Agency, was detained without trial on charges of secessionism; his detention was to last almost two years.

In addition, the Federal Government sought to undermine the economic viability of the PBS State Government. Federal revenue redirected to Sabah was reduced to the minimum level stipulated by the constitution and an arbitrary ban was imposed on logging exports from Sabah — the State's main source of independent revenue. These measures saw the State's income fall by over one-fifth from 1992 to 1993; in the period 1990 to 1993, Sabah's economy grew at only four per cent annually, compared with almost nine per cent nationally (Loh 1997).

The PBS responded with virtual capitulation, seeking re-entry into the BN and attempting to form a coalition government with its old nemesis, USNO, despite its own huge majority. The Federal Government, however, was in no mood to compromise with Pairin, stating that it was 'too late' for a reconciliation.[3] At the same time, a spate of defections by PBS leaders began, with a former State Cabinet minister and four other party stalwarts joining the BN. The PBS' position in the State Assembly was temporarily safeguarded by a State law that prevented defections by sitting Assembly members, but the regime challenged the constitutionality of that law in the Supreme Court. In an attempt to forestall this move, the PBS Government passed a second law allowing it to expel Assembly members on grounds of "indiscipline, abuse or betrayal of electorates' mandate".[4] Shortly after, the Supreme Court ruled that the original law was indeed unconstitutional and thus void.

The PBS' protection against defections gave way as its term neared conclusion. Potential cooptees could now defect to the BN, safe in the knowledge that even if they were expelled from the Assembly, they would shortly be returned on a BN ticket. After Pairin dissolved the State Assembly in January 1994, the floodgates broke. The first to go was the Deputy Chief Minister, Yong Teck Lee, who was still facing trial on illegal assembly charges; he was joined the next day by another PBS minister facing similar charges. Yong formed his own party, the Sabah Progressive Party (SAPP), which was immediately accepted into the BN. Another high-ranking PBS politician, Bernard Dompok, also left to form his own party — a resuscitation of Donald Stephens' UPKO.

For its part, the BN launched a massive election campaign based on the slogan *Sabah Baru* (or New Sabah). Vast developmentalist promises were made for infrastructural development and the construction of a university in the state — one of the PBS' key demands since its formation — if the BN was returned to power in the state (Loh 1997). At the same time, the coalition announced that UMNO itself would contest seats in Sabah, and that USNO was finally wound up. The BN slate that faced the PBS in the 1994 State elections was hence remarkably similar to the ethnic coalition that had predominated on the Peninsula — a triumvirate of ethnic parties, with UMNO contesting the Muslim-dominated seats, Dompok's UPKO contesting the non-Muslim *bumiputera* seats, and a range of smaller Chinese parties, including Yong's SAPP.

Despite the defections and the grand promises of the Federal Government, the PBS retained control of the State Assembly at the election, winning the smallest majority of twenty-five out of the forty-eight seats, although its position was improved by the presence of the six appointed members. By this time, however, the writing was on the wall for Pairin. Less than a month after the election, eight more PBS Assembly members defected and the Assembly fell to the BN. Needless to say, allegations were rife of massive bribes for the defectors; Pairin himself alleged that they were offered millions of ringgit each.[5] Political inducements also awaited the defectors. Pairin's dominance of the PBS would have assured his continuation as Chief Minister in any PBS Administration. In contrast, the BN instituted a policy of rotating the chief ministership every two years. Two of the highest profile defectors — Yong Teck Lee and Bernard Giluk Dompok — were thus both rewarded with stints as Chief Minister, together with all the financial benefits it entailed. Shortly before he took over as Chief Minister, the charges in Yong's long-delayed trial were also amended and he pleaded guilty to a lesser charge, for which he was fined a nominal 1,000 ringgit.

Following its success in wresting control of Sabah back from the PBS, the BN has largely made good on its developmentalist promises. In 1995, the new BN Administration in Sabah launched its Outline Perspective Plan Sabah (OPPS), set to run until 2010 (Sabah 1995). Although lacking detail in comparison to the national Outline Perspective Plans and Five Year Plans, it was nonetheless the first document with a long-term strategy for the State's development, since the Sabah Plan of the post-war period. The OPPS recognized that the primary sector dominance and reliance on the export of unprocessed or minimally-processed commodities was "a major structural weakness of the State's economy" (Sabah 1995, p. 13). The corrective key strategies identified were the provision of a better infrastructure and the encouragment of economic diversification, particularly in the 'downstream' processing of the State's natural resources. In the Eighth Malaysia Plan (2001–05), Federal grants to Sabah were boosted significantly, with per capita development funding allotted to Sabah doubling from 1,513 ringgit to 3,004 ringgit (Jomo and Wee 2002). Cultural grievances were also addressed, with Kadazan/Dusun language tuition introduced in schools in April 1995 (Lasimbang and Kinajil 2000) and the establishment of the long-awaited university in the state. This strategy has been rewarded with significant victories in the subsequent State elections in 1999, 2004, and 2008. Opposition parties in Sabah are now virtually moribund, garnering less than twenty per cent of the vote in 2004 and winning no seats (Lim 2004). They performed slightly better in 2008, winning 30 per cent of the votes, although this only translated into one seat. Over the same period, UMNO has also slowly increased its own control over the State Assembly, amending and then finally dropping the rotation of the chief ministership. In addition, the coalition has admitted other parties claiming to represent the non-Muslim *bumiputera*, including the PBRS (*Parti Bersatu Rakyat Sabah*, or Sabah People's United Party) and, in 2003, the PBS was finally and ingloriously allowed re-entry to the coalition, much diminished from its former position.

In the final analysis, then, the story of post-BERJAYA Sabah is one of the Federal system successfully engineering a process of political change in the State that has effectively resolved the tensions made manifest during the BERJAYA period of government. By importing UMNO as the dominant party in the State, the BN has lessened the susceptibility of the State Government to bottom-up challenges, while simultaneously devoting significant developmental funds to the State in order to lessen regionalist discontent. Islam — if not active Islamization — remains high on the agenda, with the construction of a massive new State mosque shortly after the BN took control of the Assembly, but this has been ameliorated by culturally-inclusive policies aimed at least at minimizing non-Muslim concerns; the UMNO-led State Governments have also assiduously avoided any overtly provocative policies, such as Harris' attempted appropriation of the *Kaamatan* festival. However, problems remain on the horizon. The State's economic recovery has been faltering at best, with the envisaged economic diversification largely failing to emerge, and the issue of illegal migrants continues to generate social discontent; non-citizens still make up around a quarter of the State's population. But, for the medium term at least, the Federal regime in Kuala Lumpur appears to have found a political formula that has dampened one of the most politically turbulent states of the Federation — a formula which, ironically enough, most closely, of all its predecessors, resembles the ill-fated Sabah Alliance, albeit, this time around, brought much closer to the more disciplined party structures of the national coalition.

Notes

1. *New Straits Times*, 6 November 1986.
2. *Far Eastern Economic Review*, 25 October 1990.
3. *Business Times* (Malaysia), 2 May 1992.
4. *New Straits Times*, 25 November 1992.
5. Joseph Pairin Kitingan (PBS President), interview by the author, Penampang (Sabah), 6 August 1999. Given his subsequent return to the BN, Pairin may no longer stand by these allegations.

REFERENCES

Abinales, Patricio N. *Making Mindanao: Cotabato and Davao in the Formation of the Philippine Nation-state*. Quezon City: Ateneo de Manila University Press, 2000.

Abinales, Patricio N. and Donna J. Amoroso. *State and Society in the Philippines*. Lanham, M.D.: Rowman and Littlefield, 2005.

Ahmad Ibrahim. "The Administration of Muslim Law Enactment, Sabah, 1977 (No. 15 of 1977)". *Journal of Malaysian and Comparative Law* 5, no. 2 (1978): 359–62.

Andaya, Barbara W. "Cash Cropping and Upstream-downstream Tensions: The Case of Jambi in the Seventeenth and Eighteenth Centuries". In *Southeast Asia in the Early Modern Era: Trade, Power, and Belief*, edited by Anthony Reid. Ithaca, N.Y.: Cornell University Press, 1993.

Baker, M. H. *Sabah: The First Ten Years as a Colony*. Kuala Lumpur: Malaysia Publishing House, 1965.

Black, Ian. "The Ending of Brunei Rule in Sabah, 1878–1902". *Journal of the Malayan Branch of the Royal Asiatic Society* 41, no. 2 (1968): 176–92.

———. *A Gambling Style of Government: The Establishment of Chartered Company Rule in Sabah, 1878–1915*. Kuala Lumpur: Oxford University Press, 1985.

———. "The Rundum Rebellion of 1915 in Sabah: Millenarianism and Social Protest". Paper presented at the Seminar Sejarah dan Masyarakat Sabah [Seminar on the History and Society of Sabah], Kota Kinabalu, 12–16 August 1981.

Blood, Doris E. "The Lotud". In *The Social Organization of Sabah Societies*, edited by Sherwood G. Lingenfelter. Kota Kinabalu: Sabah Museum and State Archives Department, 1990.

Brewis, Kielo S. "The Timugon Murut". In *The Social Organization of Sabah Societies*, edited by Sherwood G. Lingenfelter. Kota Kinabalu: Sabah Museum and State Archives Department, 1990.

British North Borneo. *Report on the 1951 Census*. Jesselton: Statistics Department, 1952.

———. *Report on the 1960 Census*. Jesselton: Statistics Department, 1961.

Brookfield, Harold, Lesley Potter and Yvonne Byron. *In Place of the Forest: Environmental and Socio-economic Transformation in Borneo and the Eastern Malay Peninsula*. Tokyo: United Nations University Press, 1995.

Brown, Graham K. "Restraining Autonomy: Sabah During the Mahathir Years". In *Reflections: The Mahathir Years in Malaysia*, edited by Bridget Welsh. Washington, D.C.: Johns Hopkins University School of Advanced International Studies, 2004.

———. "Playing the (Non)ethnic card: The Electoral System and Ethnic Voting Patterns in Malaysia". *Ethnopolitics* 4, no. 4 (2005): 429–45.

———. "Making Ethnic Citizens: The Politics and Practice of Education in Malaysia". *International Journal of Educational Development* 27 no. 2 (2007): 318–30.

Bumiputera Participation Unit. *Bumiputera Participation Unit's Guide Book*. Kota Kinabalu: Government Printer, n.d.

Camroux, David. "State Responses to Islamic Resurgence in Malaysia: Accommodation, Co-optation and Confrontation". *Asian Survey* 36, no. 9 (1996): 852–68.

Case, William. *Elites and Regimes in Malaysia: Revisiting a Consociational Democracy*. Clayton: Monash Asia Institute, 1996.

Chandler, G. *Agricultural Development in Sabah*. Monash Development Studies Occasional Paper, no. 1. Clayton, VIC: Monash Development Studies Centre, 1989.

Chandra Muzaffar. *Islamic Resurgence in Malaysia*. Petaling Jaya: Fajar Bakti, 1987.

Cheah Boon Kheng. *Red Star over Malaya: Resistance and Social Conflict During and After the Japanese Occupation, 1941–1946*, 3rd ed. Singapore: Singapore University Press, 2003.

———. "The Left-wing Movement in Malaya, Singapore and Borneo in the 1960s: 'An Era of Hope or Devil's Decade'?" *Inter-Asia Cultural Studies 7*, no. 4 (2006): 634–49.

Chee, Stephen. *Local Institution and Rural Development in Malaysia*. Ithaca, N.Y.: Rural Development Committee, Center for International Studies, Cornell University, 1974.

Cleary, M. C. "Plantation Agriculture and the Formulation of Native Land Rights in British North Borneo c. 1880–1930". *The Geographical Journal* 158, no. 2 (1992): 170–81.

———. "Indigenous Trade and European Economic Intervention in North-west Borneo c. 1860–1930". *Modern Asian Studies* 30, no. 2 (1996): 310–24.

Cobbold Commission. *Report of the Commission of Enquiry, North Borneo and Sarawak*. Kuala Lumpur: Jabatan Chetak Kerajaan, 1962.

Crisswell, C. N. "The Mat Salleh Rebellion Reconsidered". *Sarawak Museum Journal* 19, no. 1 (1971): 38–39.

Crocker, William M. "Notes on Sarawak and Northern Borneo". *Proceedings of the Royal Geographical Society and Monthly Record of Geography* 3, no. 4 (1881): 193–208.

Crouch, Harold. "The UMNO Crisis: 1975–77". In *Malaysian Politics and the 1978 Elections*, edited by Harold Crouch, Lee Kam Hing and Michael Ong. Kuala Lumpur: Oxford University Press, 1980.

———. *Government and Society in Malaysia*. St Leonard's, NSW: Allen and Unwin, 1996*a*.

———. "Malaysia: Do Elections Make a Difference?" In *The Politics of Elections in South East Asia*, edited by R. H. Taylor. Cambridge: Cambridge University Press, 1996*b*.

Doolittle, Amity. "Colliding Discourses: Western Land Laws and Native Customary Rights in North Borneo, 1881–1918". *Journal of Southeast Asian Studies* 34, no. 1 (2003): 97–126.

Fujio, Hara. "The 1943 Kinabalu Uprising in Sabah". In *Southeast Asian Minorities in the Wartime Japanese Empire*, edited by Paul H. Kratoska. London: RoutledgeCurzon, 2002.

Funston, N. John. *Malay Politics in Malaysia: A Study of the United Malays National Organisation and Parti Islam*. Kuala Lumpur: Heinemann Asia, 1980.

Galbraith, J. S. "The Chartering of the North Borneo Company". *The Journal of British Studies* 4, no. 2 (1965): 102–26.

Gale, Bruce. "Politics at the Periphery: A Study of the 1981 and 1982 Election Campaigns in Sabah". In *Readings in Malaysian Politics*, edited by Bruce Gale. Kuala Lumpur: Pelanduk Publications, 1986.

Glyn-Jones, Monica. *The Dusun of the Penampang Plains in North Borneo*. Canterbury: Institute of Colonial Studies, University of Kent, 1953.

Granville-Edge, P. J. *The Sabahan: The Life and Death of Tun Fuad Stephens*. Petaling Jaya: Writers' Publishing House, 2002.

Gudgeon, Peter S. "Economic Development in Sabah, 1881–1981". In *Commemorative History of Sabah, 1881–1981*, edited by Anwar Sullivan and Cecilia Leong. Kota Kinabalu: Sabah State Government Centenary Publications Committee, 1981.

Gullick, J. M. *Malay Society in the Late Nineteenth Century*. Singapore: Oxford University Press, 1989.

Hall, Kenneth R. "Upstream and Downstream Unification in Southeast Asia's First Islamic Polity: The Changing Sense of Community in the Fifteenth Century Hikayat Raja-Raja Pasai Court Chronicle". *Journal of the Economic and Social History of the Orient* 44, no. 2 (2001): 198–229.

Hamayotsu, Kikue. "The Politics of Syariah Reform: The Making of the State Religio-legal Apparatus". In *Malaysia: Islam, Society and Politics*, edited by Virginia Matheson Hooker and Norani Othman. Singapore: Institute of Southeast Asian Studies, 2003.

Han Sin Fong. "A Constitutional Coup d'Etat: An Analysis of the Birth and Victory of the BERJAYA Party in Sabah, Malaysia". *Asian Survey* 19, no. 4 (1979): 379–89.

Harris Mohd. Salleh. *Ikrar Pemimpin-Pemimpin Parti Berjaya*. Kota Kinabalu: Sabah State Government, Jabatan Ketua Menteri no. 41, 1981.

Harris, Sue. "The Tagal Murut". In *The Social Organization of Sabah Societies*, edited by Sherwood G. Lingenfelter. Kota Kinabalu: Sabah Museum and State Archives Department, 1990.

Harrison, Tom. "The Advent of Islam to West and North Borneo". *Journal of the Malayan Branch of the Royal Asiatic Society* 45, no. 1 (1973): 10–20.

Horowitz, Donald L. *Ethnic Groups in Conflict.* Berkeley: University of California Press, 1985.

———. "The Qur'an and the Common Law: Islamic Law Reform and the Theory of Legal Change". *The American Journal of Comparative Law* 42, no. 2 (1994): 233–93.

Hussin Mutalib. *Islam and Ethnicity in Malay Politics.* Kuala Lumpur: Oxford University Press, 1991.

Ismail Haji Ibrahim. "Dakwah Islamiah Di Malaysia" [Islamic Proselytization in Malaysia]. Paper presented at the Seminar Kebangsaan Konsep Pembangunan Dalam Islam [National Seminar on the Concept of Development in Islam], Universiti Kebangsaan Malaysia, Bangi, 10–12 March 1981.

Ismail Yusoff. *Politik dan Agama di Sabah* [Politics and Religion in Sabah]. Bangi: Penerbit Universiti Kebangsaan Malaysia, 2004.

Jabatan Ketua Menteri. *Jawatan Kuasa Kemajuan Kampung* [Village Development Committees]. Kota Kinabalu: Pusat Pembangunan Masyarakat Sabah, Jabatan Ketua Menteri, 1975.

Jomo, K. S. and Wee Cong Hui. *The Political Economy of Malaysian Federalism: Economic Development, Public Policy and Conflict Containment.* Helsinki: United Nations University/World Institute for Development Economics Research Discussion Paper, 2002.

Kahin, Audrey R. "Crisis on the Periphery: The Rift Between Kuala Lumpur and Sabah". *Pacific Affairs* 65, no. 1 (1992): 30–49.

Kahin, George McT. "The State of North Borneo, 1881–1946". *The Far Eastern Quarterly* 7, no. 1 (1947): 43–65.

Kathirithamby-Wells, J. and John Villiers, eds. *The Southeast Asian Port and Polity: Rise and Demise.* Singapore: Singapore University Press, 1990.

Kaur, Amarjit. *Economic Change in East Malaysia: Sabah and Sarawak since 1850.* Basingstoke: MacMillan, 1998.

Khoo Boo Teik. "Limits to Democracy: Political Economy, Ideology, and Ruling Coalition". In *Elections and Democracy in Malaysia*, edited by Norani Othman and Mavis Puthucheary. Bangi: Penerbit Universiti Kebangsaan Malaysia, 2005.

Khoo Khay Jin. "The Grand Vision: Mahathir and Modernisation". In *Fragmented Vision: Culture and Politics in Contemporary Malaysia*, edited by Joel S. Kahn and Francis Loh Kok Wah. Honolulu: University of Hawaii Press, 1992.

Kitingan, Joseph P. *PBS Government Policies on the Civil Servants in Sabah.* Kota Kinabalu: Chief Minister's Department, 1985.

Laporan Banci Penduduk 1970, Negeri Sabah [Report of the Population Census 1970, Sabah State]. Kota Kinabalu: Jabatan Perangkaan Malaysia, Negeri Sabah, 1971.

Laporan Peruntukan Negeri Dan Persekutuan Bagi Projek-projek Kecil Luar Bandar, Tahun 1978–1979 [Report on federal and state allocation for small projects in rural areas, 1978–1979]. Kota Kinabalu: Kerajaan Negeri Sabah, 1980.

Lasimbang, Claudia. "Indigenous Peoples of Sabah: Traditional Resource Management". Paper delivered at the Indigenous Rights in the Commonwealth Project, South and Southeast Asia regional experts meeting, New Delhi 2002.

Lasimbang, Rita and Trixie Kinajil. "Changing the Language Ecology of Kadazandusun: The Role of the Kadazandusun Language Foundation". *Current Issues in Language Planning* 1, no. 3 (2000): 415–23.

Lieberman, Victor. "Local Integration and Eurasian Analogies: Structuring Southeast Asian History, c.1350–c.1830". *Modern Asian Studies* 27 (1993): 475–572.

Lijphart, Arend. *Democracy in Plural Societies: A Comparative Exploration*. New Haven: Yale University Press, 1977.

Lim, G. "Back to the Future? The 2004 Election in Sabah". *Aliran Monthly* 24, no. 3 (2004).

Lim Hong Hai. "Sabah and Sarawak in Malaysia: The Real Bargain, or, what have they got themselves into?" *Kajian Malaysia* 15, no. 1/2 (1997): 15–56.

Loh Kok Wah, Francis. "Modernisation, Cultural Revival and Counter-hegemony: The Kadazans of Sabah in the 1980s". In *Fragmented Vision: Culture and Politics in Contemporary Malaysia*, edited by Joel S. Kahn and Francis Loh Kok Wah. Honolulu: University of Hawaii Press, 1992.

———. "'Sabah Baru' Dan Pujukan Pembangunan: Penyelesaikan Hubungan Persekutuan-negeri Dalam Malaysia" ['Sabah Baru' and the Spell of Development: Resolving Federal-state Relations in Malaysia]. *Kajian Malaysia* 15, no. 1/2 (1997): 175–99.

———. "Electoral Politics in Sabah, 1999: Gerrymandering, "phantoms", and the 3Ms". In *New Politics in Malaysia*, edited by Francis Loh Kok Wah and Johan Saravanamuttu. Singapore: Institute of Southeast Asian Studies, 2003.

Luping, Herman J. "The Formation of Malaysia Revisited". In *Sabah 25 Years Later, 1963–1988*, edited by Jeffrey G. Kitingan and Maximus J. Ongkili. Kota Kinabalu: Institute for Development Studies, 1989.

———. *Sabah's Dilemma: The Political History of Sabah, 1960–1994*. Kuala Lumpur: Magnus Books, 1994.

Maguin, Pierre-Yves. "The Merchant and the King: Political Myths of Southeast Asian Coastal Polities". *Indonesia* 52 (October 1991): 41–54.

Malaysia. *Second Malaysia Plan, 1971–1976*. Kuala Lumpur: Penchetak Nasional, 1971.

———. *Fourth Malaysia Plan, 1981–1985*. Kuala Lumpur: Government Printer, 1981.

———. *Fifth Malaysia Plan, 1986–1990*. Kuala Lumpur: Government Printer, 1986.

———. *Sixth Malaysia Plan, 1991–1995*. Kuala Lumpur: Government Printer, 1991.

Mandal, Sumit. "Transethnic Solidarities, Racialisation and Social Equality". In *The State of Malaysia: Ethnicity, Equity and Reform*, edited by Edmund Terence Gomez. London: RoutledgeCurzon, 2004.

Mauzy, Diane K. and R. S. Milne. "The Mahathir Administration in Malaysia: Discipline through Islam". *Pacific Affairs* 56, no. 4 (1983): 617–48.

McKenna, Thomas M. *Muslim Rulers and Rebels: Everyday Politics and Armed Separatism in the Southern Philippines*. Berkeley: University of California Press, 1998.

Means, Gordon P. "Eastern Malaysia: The Politics of Federalism". *Asian Survey* 8, no. 4 (1968): 289–308.

———. *Malaysian Politics: The Second Generation*. Singapore: Oxford University Press, 1991.

Milne, R. S. "Patrons, Clients and Ethnicity: The Case of Sarawak and Sabah in Malaysia". *Asian Survey* 13, no. 10 (1973): 891–907.

———. "Malaysia and Singapore in 1974". *Asian Survey* 15, no. 2 (1975).

Milne, R. S. and K. J. Ratnam. "Patterns and Peculiarities of Voting in Sabah, 1967". *Asian Survey* 9, no. 5 (1969): 373–81.

———. *Malaysia — New States in a New Nation: Political Development of Sarawak and Sabah in Malaysia*. London: Frank Cass, 1974.

Milner, Anthony C. *Kerajaan: Malay Political Culture on the Eve of Colonial Rule*. Tucson, AZ: University of Arizona Press, 1982.

Nagata, Judith. *The Reflowering of Malaysian Islam: Modern Religious Radicals and Their Roots*. Vancouver: University of British Columbia Press, 1984.

North Borneo. "Annual Report 1949". Jesselton, 1949.

———. "Annual Report 1951". Jesselton, 1951.

———. "Annual Report 1960". Jesselton, 1960.

———. "Annual Report 1961". Jesselton, 1961.

———. "Annual Report 1962". Jesselton, 1962.

Ong, Michael. "The Democratic Action Party and the 1978 General Election". In *Malaysian Politics and the 1978 Election*, edited by Harold Crouch, Lee Kam Hing and Michael Ong. Kuala Lumpur: Oxford University Press, 1980.

Ongkili, James P. *Modernization in East Malaysia 1960–1970*. Kuala Lumpur: Oxford University Press, 1972.

———. "Historical Background". In *Commemorative History of Sabah: 1881–1981*, edited by Anwar Sullivan and Cecila Leong. Kuala Lumpur: Sabah State Government Centenary Publications Committee, 1981.

———. *Nation-building in Malaysia, 1946–1974*. Singapore: Oxford University Press, 1985.

Outline Perspective Plan Sabah 1995–2010. Kota Kinabalu: Pencetak Kerajaan Sabah, 1995.

Pang Teck Wei. "Economic Growth and Development in Sabah: 25 years After Independence". In *Sabah 25 Years Later, 1963–1988*, edited by Jeffrey G. Kitingan and Maximus J. Ongkili. Kota Kinabalu, Sabah: Institute for Development Studies, 1988.

———. "The Making of a Development Plan for Sabah: Issues, Problems, Solutions". Paper delivered at the Borneo Research Council Seminar on Change and Development, Kuching, 4–9 August 1990.

Paridah Abd. Samad and Darulsalam Abu Bakar. "Malaysia-Philippines Relations: The Issue of Sabah". *Asian Survey* 32, no. 6 (1992): 554–67.

Pringle, R. *Rajahs and Rebels: The Ibans of Sarawak under Brooke Rule, 1841–1941*. London: Macmillan, 1974.

Pryer, William B. "Notes on North-Eastern Borneo and the Sulu Islands". *Proceedings of the Royal Geographical Society and Monthly Record of Geography* 5, no. 3 (1883): 90–96.

Pugh-Kitingan, Jacqueline. "Cultural Development in Sabah, 1963–1988". In *Sabah: 25 Years Later, 1963–1988*, edited by Jeffrey G. Kitingan and Maximus J. Ongkili. Kota Kinabalu: Institute for Development Studies, 1989.

Puthucheary, Mavis. *Federalism at the Crossroads: The 1985 Elections in Sabah and their Implications for Federal-State Relations*. Singapore: Institute of Strategic and International Studies, 1985.

Raffaele, Paul. *Harris Salleh of Sabah*. Hong Kong: Condor Publishing, 1986.

Ramanathan, Kalimuthu. "The Sabah State Elections of April 1985". *Asian Survey* 26, no. 7 (1986): 815–37.

Ranjit Singh, D. S. "Sistem Politik Pribumi Sabah". [The Indigenous Political System in Sabah]. *Malaysia dari Segi Sejarah* 9 (1980).

———. "Brunei and the Hinterland of Sabah: Commercial and Economic Relations, with Special Reference to the Second Half of the Nineteenth Century". In *The Southeast Asian Port and Polity: Rise and Demise*, edited by J. Kathirithamby-Wells and John Villiers. Singapore: Singapore University Press, 1990.

———. *The Making of Sabah, 1865–1941*. Kuala Lumpur: University of Malaya Press, 2000.

Reid, Anthony. "Islamization and Christianization in Southeast Asia: The Critical Phase, 1550–1650". In *Southeast Asia in the Early Modern Era: Trade, Power and Belief*, edited by Anthony Reid. Ithaca, N.Y.: Cornell University Press, 1993.

Roff, William R. "Patterns of Islamization in Malaysia, 1890s–1990s: Exemplars, Institutions and Vectors". *Journal of Islamic Studies* 9, no. 2 (1998): 210–28.

Rooney, J. *Khabar Gembira: A History of the Catholic Church in East Malaysia and Brunei (1880–1976)*. London and Kota Kinabalu: Burns and Oates/Mill Hill Missionaries, 1981.

Ross-Larson, Bruce, ed. *Sabah and the Sabah Foundation*. Kota Kinabalu: Sabah Foundation, 1974.

Saint John, Spenser. *Rajah Brooke: The Englishman as Ruler of an Eastern State*. London… Fisher Unwin, 1869.

Shamsul, A. B. "The Economic Dimension of Malay Nationalism: The Socio-historical Roots of the New Economic Policy and its Contemporary Implications". *The Developing Economies* 35, no. 3 (1997): 240–61.

Smith, Anthony D. *Myths and Memories of the Nation*. Oxford: Oxford University Press, 1999.

Stark, M. T. and S. J. Allen. "The Transition to History in Southeast Asia: An Introduction". *International Journal of Historical Archeology* 2, no. 3 (1998): 163–74.

Stockwell, Anthony J. "Introduction". In *Malaysia*, edited by Anthony J. Stockwell. London: HMSO, 2004.

Sutherland, Helen. "Slavery and the Slave Trade in South Sulawesi, 1660–1800s". In *Slavery, Bondage and Dependency in Southeast Asia*, edited by Anthony Reid. St. Lucia: University of Queensland Press, 1983.

Sutton, Keith. "Malaysia's FELDA Land Settlement Model in Time and Space". *Geoforum* 20 (1989): 339–54.

Syed Husin Ali. "Patterns of Rural Leadership in Malaya". *Journal of the Malayan Branch of the Royal Asiatic Society* 41, no. 1 (1968): 95–145.

Tanaka, T. *Hidden Horrors: Japanese War Crimes in World War II*. Oxford: Westview Press, 1998. Original edition, 1996.

Tarling, Nicholas. *Britain, the Brookes, and Brunei*. Kuala Lumpur: Oxford University Press, 1971.

———. *Sulu and Sabah*. Kuala Lumpur: Oxford University Press, 1978.

———. *A Sudden Rampage: The Japanese Occupation of Southeast Asia, 1941–1945*. London: Hurst and Company, 2001.

Tilman, Robert O. "Malaysia: The Problems of Federation". *The Western Political Quarterly* 16, no. 4 (1963): 897–911.

———. "Mustapha's Sabah, 1968–1975: The Tun Steps Down". *Asian Survey* 16, no. 6 (1976): 495–509.

Tregonning, K. G. "The Elimination of Slavery in North Borneo". *Journal of the Malayan Branch of the Royal Asiatic Society* 26, no. 1 (1953).

———. "William Pryer, the Founder of Sandakan". *Journal of the Malayan Branch of the Royal Asiatic Society* 27, no. 1 (1954): 36–50.

———. "The Mat Salleh Revolt, 1894–1905". *Journal of the Malayan Branch of the Royal Asiatic Society* 29, no. 1 (1956): 20–36.

———. *A History of Modern Sabah (North Borneo, 1881–1961)*. Singapore: University of Malaya Press, 1965.

Walker, J. H. *Power and Prowess: The Origins of Brooke Kingship in Sarawak*. Honolulu: University of Hawaii Press, 2002.

Warren, James F. *Iranun and Balangingi: Globalization, Maritime Raiding and the Birth of Ethnicity*. Singapore: Singapore University Press, 2002.

Weber, Max. *From Max Weber*. New York: Galaxy, 1946.

William, V. Gabriel. "The General State Administration of Sabah, 1881–1981". In *Commemorative History of Sabah, 1991–1981*, edited by Anwar Sullivan and Cecilia Leong. Kuala Lumpur: Sabah State Government Centenary Publications Committee, 1981.

Wolters, O. W. "Southeast Asia as a Southeast Asian Field of Study". *Indonesia* 58 (1994): 1–17.

———. *History, Culture, and Region in Southeast Asian Perspectives*. Ithaca, N.Y.: Cornell Southeast Asia Program, 1999.

Wong Tze-Ken, Danny. *The Transformation of an Immigrant Society: A Study of the Chinese in Sabah*. London: ASEAN Academic Press, 1998.

———. "Anti-Japanese Activities in North Borneo before World War II: 1937–1941". *Journal of Southeast Asian Studies* 32, no. 1 (2001): 93–106.

Wookey, W. K. "The Mat Salleh Rebellion". *Sarawak Museum Journal* 7, no. 8 (1956): 193–201.

Wright, Leigh R. *The Origins of British Borneo*. Hong Kong: Hong Kong University Press, 1970.

INDEX

ABOUT THE AUTHOR

A native Sabahan, Regina Lim has studied Sociology and Political Science at the University of Warwick, UK and Universiti Sains Malaysia, and is currently conducting doctoral research at the University of Birmingham, UK. She has worked for the Political Studies Association of the UK and has been a researcher and translator for international comparative projects based at the University of Oxford, Universiti Kebangsaan Malaysia, and the School of Oriental and African Studies, University of London.

www.ingramcontent.com/pod-product-compliance
Lightning Source LLC
Chambersburg PA
CBHW021540260326
41914CB00001B/87

* 9 7 8 9 8 1 2 3 0 8 1 2 2 *